T0319212

Ethnic Groups of the Senegambia Region

Ethnic Groups of the Senegambia Region

A Brief History

Patience Sonko – Godwin

Sunrise Publishers Ltd.

P.O. Box 955

Banjul, The Gambia

First published 1985
Second Edition 1988
Reprinted 1994
Third Edition 2003
Reprinted 2019

Cover Illustration: Depicts some peoples of the Senegambia Region in the precolonial and colonial periods and instruments of the oral historians.

ISBN 978 9983 9900 6 5

CONTENTS

List of Illustrations vi

Acknowledgements vii

Introduction 1

The Mandinka.. 3

TheWolof 19

The Serer 32

The Fula 42

The Tukulor 54

The Serahule 60

The Jola 68

ILLUSTRATIONS

Fig. 1 A Mandinka Man   10

Fig. 2 A Mandinka Kora Player   11

Fig. 3 A Wolof Man   21

Fig. 4 A Wolof Woman   21

Fig. 5 A Serer Woman and Baby   36

Fig. 6 A Young Fula Girl   44

Fig. 7 A Fula Woman   46

Fig. 8 A Tukulor Woman   56

Fig. 9 A Tukulor Man   58

Fig. 10 A Serahule Woman   65

Fig. 11 A Jola Woman   72

MAPS : Map 1 Ethnic Distribution in the Senegambia Region   viii

Map 2 Early Mandinka Kingdoms   6

Map 3 The Kaabu Empire   9

Map 4 The Jolof Empire   22

Map 5 Serer States of Sine and Saloum   35

Map 6 The patterns of Fula Migration   45

Map 7 Serahule Migration into The Gambia   63

Map 8 Some Major and Minor Jola Groups, Settlements and Towns   71

ACKNOWLEDGEMENTS

The author and publishers wish to thank the following for their help with illustrations and information:

The Gambia National Archives

Archives Nationales, Dakar, Senegal

IFAN, Dakar, Senegal

Gambia National Insurance Company

Gambia National Museum

Oral Histories Division, Banjul

Department of Youth, Sports and Culture

and all those who have contributed to making this publication a welcome addition to local publishing efforts.

Map I. Distribution of the Major Ethnic Groups of the Senegambia Region

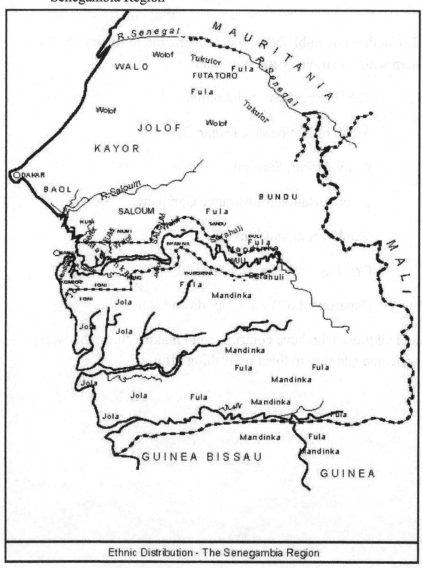

Ethnic Distribution - The Senegambia Region

INTRODUCTION

This book is about the history of the major ethnic groups of the Senegambia Region in pre-colonial times. It deals with the origin, migration, state and empire formations, if any, and finally with the disintegration and or subjugation of these groups by outsiders. It therefore aims at providing a basic but essential knowledge of the peoples of the area before and after the arrival of the Europeans. Thus, it will prove invaluable to children of the region and readers who are interested in the historical developments of the area. The book also helps to address and disprove the generally held view that Africa had no history prior to the coming of the Europeans.

The two independent states of Senegal and The Gambia are located in the Senegambia Region which is bounded on the north by the Republic of Mauritania, along the course of the River Senegal, on the east by the Republic of Mali, on the south by the Republics of Guinea and Guinea-Bissau and on the west by the Atlantic Ocean. Together the two independent states cover an area of approximately 207,200 square kilometres.

Senegal overwhelms The Gambia with her size and position. It is about 196,000 sq. km. in area, whereas The Gambia is only 11,000 sq. km. The Gambia is surrounded by Senegal on the north, east and south, and in the west; faces the Atlantic Ocean. Thus, The Gambia has been described as 'an arrow through a heart', for she divides Senegal into two unequal parts. Though landlocked with the exception of the western part, The Gambia has the distinct feature of having the most navigable river in West Africa. The 'golden river' that meanders through the length of the country makes all parts of it easily accessible and serviceable.

This book is entitled Ethnic Groups of The Senegambia Region: A Brief History and not Ethnic Groups of The Gambia because of the fact that the histories of the independent states of Senegal and The Gambia are interrelated. Although these states have different official languages, monetary and educational systems, they share the same ethnic groups, religions, culture and traditions.

The word Senegambia, is not new. It was used as early as 1765 by the British to refer to the French settlements of Gorée Island and St Louis in

1

Senegal and the British settlement of James Island in The Gambia, under their administration. Its usage became more common with the establishment of the Confederation of Senegal and The Gambia on 1 February 1982. But the Senegambian Confederation was a marriage of convenience and therefore faced many difficulties. It collapsed in August 1989. Despite this failure the governments of Senegal and The Gambia realised the close affinity of the peoples of the two states and have continued to work for closer cooperation for these reasons Senegambia is an apt word for the title of the book.

In 1983, the national histories of member countries of the West African Examinations Council (WAEC), of which The Gambia is a member, were launched as a requirement for candidates of the history examination. Since there have been renewed efforts in many African countries to reassess and rewrite their histories, historians of the Council were aware of the felt need to promote the history of West Africa and to help dispel certain misconceptions and enigmas that have been prevalent over the years. This book is one of many which will help Gambian candidates to answer the first part of the National History paper.

I wish to draw students' attention to the fact that both major and minor ethnic groups have contributed to the historical developments of the Senegambia Region.

The decision on which groups to include was determined by:

(a)   the quantity and quality of information, both oral and written, that was collected during the research.

(b)   the present population of the group in the Senegambia Region – the larger the group, the better its eligibility for being included in the text; and

(c)   the requirements of the National History syllabus.

However, mention of some minor groups is made in places where they relate to the issue in question.

2

1

THE MANDINKA

The Mandinka are sometimes referred to as Mandingo or Malinke. Today they are widely dispersed in West Africa and are found in great numbers in countries such as Guinea, Guinea-Bissau, Mali and especially in the Senegambia Region. Mandinka settlements could be viewed as forming a triangle from the Senegambia Region at the base and Niger at the top.

ORIGIN AND MIGRATION

The Mandinka who settled in the Senegambia Region were originally from Kangaba (or Manding), a state in the ancient Empire of Mali. This is believed to be the original home of the Mandinka and was a vassal of the emperor of ancient Ghana, the first Empire of the Western Sudan. Ghana was destroyed by the Almoravids in 1076, and Kangaba became a vassal of the Susu state of Kaniaga, the successor state of Ghana. This vassalage was short-lived, for in 1235, Kangaba gained her independence from the powerful but ruthless King of the Susu, Sumanguru Konteh. This feat was achieved by the illustrious and renowned Mandinka leader, Sundiata Keita (or Mari Jatta). He was later responsible for laying the foundation of the Mali Empire and for the Mandinka greatness and expansion into the rest of West Africa, especially into the Senegambia Region.

It is strongly believed that Mandinka expansion and migration into the Senegambia Region had begun even before the existence of the Mali Empire. Migrants had moved in small groups from the area of the ancient Mali Empire in search of better farmland, then settled and intermarried with the indigenous inhabitants of the lower regions of

3

Senegambia and Guinea-Bissau. A larger group of migrants was led by Tiramang Traore (Tarawally), a general of Sundiata Keita. Both the major and minor migrations, which took place between the former Mali Empire and the Senegambia Region, were influenced by this search for better farmland. To this end the movements of traders and hunters to the vast but sparsely populated and well-watered land to the west of Mali were quite frequent. However, this region had a more favourable climate than that of Mali. The local inhabitants of the lower Senegambia Region were poorly organised and were therefore easily defeated by the powerful Mandinka army. This situation in fact gave the people of Mali a greater desire to migrate. The migrants had the added incentive of greater trade opportunities in this area. The Mali Empire had become wealthy because of its participation in the trans-Saharan trade. Consequently, the Mandinka migrants hoped to become even richer in this region, where they had no competitors. Finally, these migrations gave young princes and generals, who unfortunately could not become rulers or even governors in the provinces of Mali, the opportunity to have their own territories which they could rule in the name of Mali.

The great migration from the Mali Region to the Senegambia Region occurred during the reign of Sundiata Keita, and was led by one of his generals known as Tiramang or Tiramangan Traore (Tarawally). He was to conquer a large part of the area, which later became Guinea-Bissau and the Kassa (Casa)Region (now the Casamance region in Senegal) in the lower Senegambia Region. However before going on the main mission for Mali, Tiramang was sent on a punitive expedition against the Kingdom of Jolof, in the northeast of present day Senegal. The Jolof ruler had not only refused to sell horses to Sundiata, which he needed for the expedition, but killed his messengers as well. MANDINKA

Tiramang left Mali by the mid-thirteenth century with over 75,000 settlers, including princes, generals, marabouts, free men, different artisan groups and slaves. He proceeded to Jolof, defeated and killed the

4

ruler, and then went on to conquer the Kassa Region. In his efforts to conquer the region he was helped by Mandinka families who had settled much earlier in the area. The most prominent of these was the Sanneh family. This conquest forced the migration of some of the local inhabitants, such as the Jola and Bainounka, towards The Gambia and the Atlantic coast. He proceeded to build the Kaabu Empire which became the home of thousands of Mandinka. The capital of Kaabu was Kansala. The empire lasted until the 1860s when it was destroyed by the Fula of Futa Jalon in Guinea.

THE KAABU EMPIRE

The Kassa Region became the nucleus of what later came to be known as the Kaabu Empire. Tiramang first married one of the daughters of the Sanneh family and had several children with her. He later continued his conquests, gradually defeating the people who lived in the area or occupying the vacant land of most of The Gambia Region, Middle and Upper Casamance, and the northern part of Guinea-Bissau. By the end of the thirteenth century, the Mandinka were in control of the land which stretched from The Gambia to the base of Futa Jalon to the southeast in the modern state of Guinea. Each newly conquered area had a group of settlers who were ruled by one of Tiramang's sons or generals. In some cases the Mandinka settled among the local inhabitants and intermarried with them.

Unfortunately, Tiramang never returned to Mali, for he died in Basse in Upper Gambia. However, it was because of this migration from Mali that many Mandinka families ended up in The Gambia, Casamance, and Guinea Bissau and are able to link their ancestry to the founder of the Kaabu Empire, Tiramang, or to some of the people who accompanied him on his epic journey. Thus, the Sanyang of Kantora, the Contehs (or Kontehs) of the Kombos in The Gambia, the Bojangs and Jasseys (or Jassis) all claim their ancestry directly or indirectly from the Ancient Mali Empire. Until the fall of the Mali Empire, Kaabu remained the most important vassal state. Some of the rulers of the states of the Kaabu Empire even got the authority to rule from their ancestral home, Mali. Some of the early states of Kaabu were Jimara, Tumanna, Kantora, Sankolla, Sama, Pachana, and Wuropana (or Eropina).

5

Not all Mandinka kingdoms were under the political domination of the Kaabu Empire. Kombo was originally a Jola state which went to the Mandinka by right of conquest. The Mandinka were helped by an army sent by the Emperor of Kaabu. The victory over the Jola and other

nkuto (a joking

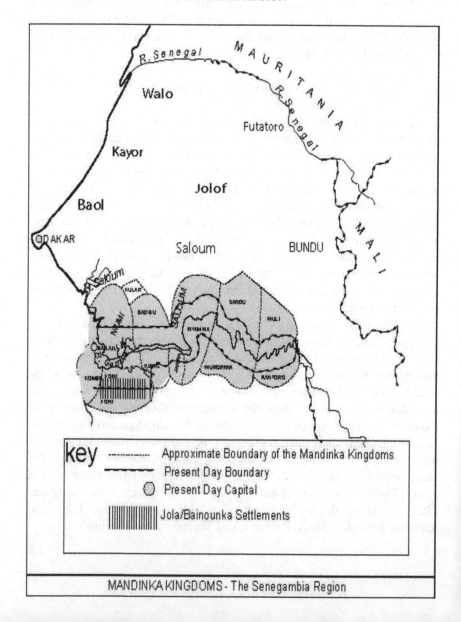

key
--------- Approximate Boundary of the Mandinka Kingdoms
———— Present Day Boundary
◯ Present Day Capital
▓▓▓▓▓ Jola/Bainounka Settlements

MANDINKA KINGDOMS - The Senegambia Region

Map 2 - Mandinka

MANDINKA

relationship) between the people of Kaabu and those of Kombo. This joking relationship meant that the two parties swore to support each other in times of trouble, mediate on behalf of each other without causing offences, and intermarry. The alliance was binding even to unborn generations, and anyone who broke it was subjected to a terrible curse. This type of alliance existed among various Mandinka states. Niumi, on the north bank and Jarra, on the south bank of the River Gambia had such an agreement.

NYANCHO AND KORINGSTATES

The *Nyanchos* and *Korings* were members of the ruling class of the Kaabu Empire and some of their vassal states. The Nyanchos and Korings traced their descent from Tiramang through the paternal line. According to tradition, the Nyanchos were children born from the marriage between one of the sons of Tiramang and a mysterious woman called Balaba. No one knew where she came from, but she lived in a cave for several years before she was discovered by a hunter. Balaba was always in white and came out only at night. After her discovery, she married one of Tiramang's sons. They had four daughters who were also believed to have supernatural powers.

Three of these children married the Mandinka rulers of Jimara, Sama and Pachana, which were among the states of the Kaabu Empire. The fourth daughter married the ruler of the Serer state of Saloum. All the descendants of these four children of Balaba came to be known as Nyanchos.

The emperors of the Empire of Kaabu were from that time chosen from the states of Jimara, Sama and Pachana in rotation. Claimants to the thrones of these states and to the emperorship of Kaabu could only rule if they could trace their right through a female Nyancho. Thus, the system of inheritance in these states was matrilineal. A state that was ruled by a Nyancho was known as a Nyancho state.

The Korings also became another group of the ruling class and
ere known as Korings.
Since these young princes could not become rulers of states by tracing
their descent through their fathers, they invariably became governors of
provinces. Another group of nobles who were considered Korings were
the members of powerful Mandinka families who had allied with the
founding ruling lineages of Kaabu. Yet other Korings were children the
emperors had with women who were not Nyanchos. These groups of
nobility could never became Nyanchos or rule, but their children could
claim the title if their mothers were Nyanchos. Some Nyanchos too,
who had no opportunity of ruling embarked on quests to establish their
own kingdoms. Korings who were not content with the mere office of
governor moved out and founded their own states that became known as
Koring states. This desire by Nyanchos and Korings to found their own
states was largely responsible for the large number of Mandinka in the
Senegambia Region.

By the mid-seventeenth century, Mali had long ceased to exist in the
east and had been replaced by the Songhai Empire. However, Kaabu
remained the most important empire in the Senegambia Region. During
this period, Mandinka civilisation reached its highest point. The *kora*, a
twenty-one-stringed musical instrument, that was the main instrument
used by the Mandinka praise-singers and oral historians, was
introduced. It is still used in the Senegambia Region, Mali, Guinea and
Guinea-Bissau. The older instruments of Mali like the *balafon*
(xylophone), *kontingo* (a three-stringed instrument), and the *bolombato*
(a gourd harp) are still in use too. Masquerades like the *kankurang*, the
mamoo and the *tinirinya* all originated from Kaabu and have continued
to be the pride of the Mandinka.

MANDINKA KINGDOMS

As stated earlier, migrations led to the founding of many states and
kingdoms, some of which were located on both the north and south
banks of the River Gambia but extended well beyond the present
boundary of this country into Senegal. Some were founded in Southern
Casamance. Today some of these ancient places such as Wuli, Baddibu,

and Niumi, bear their original names. The positions of these kingdoms located in The Gambia Region, moving from the east to the west, were as follows:

MANDINKA

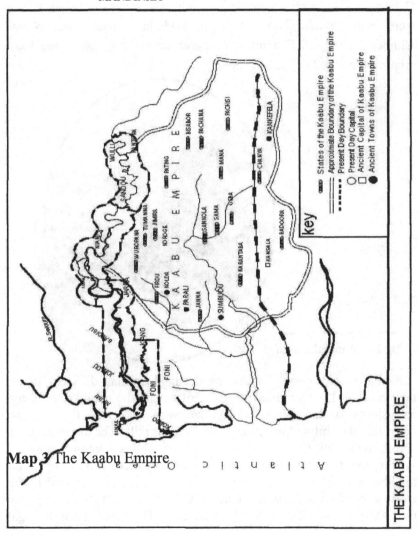

Map 3 The Kaabu Empire

The states on the south bank were Kantora, Tumanna, Jimara, Wuropana, Nyamina, Jarra, Kiang, Foni and Kombo. Foni, which was occupied by the Jola and Bainounka, remained independent of Kaabu, but was later incorporated with the other Gambian kingdoms to form the Colony of The Gambia under British rule. The states on the north bank were Wuli, Sandu, Niani, Saloum, Baddibu, Jokadu, and Niumi. Although Sine and Saloum were Serer states, they had some loose relationship with the Kaabu Empire.

Fig 1 A Mandinka man

As the various people settled on the land forming different states, they continued the stratified structure of having the nobility at the top and slaves at the bottom. Free men, who were also the farmers, cultivated the soil and produced corn, *coos* or millet for the inhabitants and for home use. Cotton was also produced. Slaves were owned by the nobility and free men and played a major role in food production. With the abolition of slavery and the slave trade many men engaged in the cultivation of groundnuts that became the cash crop of the country. By the 1880s almost all the Mandinka states in The Gambia and Senegal were producing groundnuts in large quantities. Women were engaged in rice production. They did not own land.

Cattle were mostly owned by the rulers and nobility and Fula herders tended these animals. The Mandinka also kept sheep, goats and chickens. In areas where the states were near the sea and allowed for fluvial salt production like Niumi and Kiang, mainly women produced the salt. Artisans such as leather workers produced leather, black smiths produced farming implements and weavers produced cloths. Specific families carried out these specific jobs. Some men were also engaged in hunting and fishing and certain other families were the traders (*juula* or *dyula*) exchanging goods from one state to the other and with the Europeans.

Fig 2 A Mandinka Kora Player (Jali).

The *griots* (or *jali*) continued to be the keepers of the states and families' histories, handing down vital information to younger generations of their families. Thus today we are able to have the histories of the various states. The Gambian kingdoms were sometimes ruled by a single lineage or *kaabiiloo*, as it was known among the Mandinka. Thus, Wuli was ruled by the Wali Kaabiiloo, Sankolla by the Sonko Kaabiiloo, and Kantora by the Sanyang Kaabiiloo. On the other hand, some states were ruled by three or four lineages that rotated the kingship among them. Niumi, located at the mouth of the River Gambia, was engaged in this kind of rulership. It was governed in turn

11

by the Jammeh, Manneh and Sonko Kaabiiloolu (plural). Originally, this state was ruled by the Jammehs who later invited the Mannehs of Kaabu to share kingship with them. The Sonko only had a share in running this state because they helped the ruler gain his independence from Saloum. But when the British took over Niumi in the late 1880s, the Sonko became the permanent rulers of this state.

Rotating the kingship had its problems. Some rulers refused to relinquish power to the next lineage, while others usurped power from the weaker lineages of kings, even when they had no right to the throne. In the kingdom of Tumanna which was on the south bank of the River Gambia, for example, the king's son secretly ruled for many years without informing the people of his father's death, just because he wanted to ensure that power remained with his family. In Kansala, the capital of Kaabu, the King of Sama refused to hand over power to the King of Pachana whose turn it was to become emperor. This led to a war in which the King of Sama was defeated. Although there were many such reports of violations of the rule of succession, many Mandinka states followed the rule to ensure peace. Joking relationships helped to maintain peace among many states.

At the same time there were many wars between neighbouring states. The best known of such wars was that between Jokadu and Niumi, in which a brave prince called Kelefa Sanneh met his death. The Gambian kingdoms eventually lost their independence to the British, and they remained subjected to them until The Gambia was granted independence in 1965.

THE FALL OF KAABU

The Kaabu Empire fell because it suffered a major invasion by the Fula (or Peul) from the Futa Jalon in 1868. Before this time, Kaabu had experienced waves of migration of Fula coming from the neighbouring states of Bundu, Futa Toro and Futa Jalon. The Fula were attracted by the fertile and well-watered land of Kaabu, which they needed for their cattle. However, they suffered many injustices from their overlords, the Mandinka rulers, and this resulted in deep resentment, which was further aggravated by the fact that the people of Kaabu followed the traditional African religions while most of the Fula were Muslims.

12

Although there were some Mandinka Muslims who were converted by itinerant traders, the main population remained faithful to the traditional religion. Those Fula who remained traditional worshippers felt alienated from the Mandinka religion because they had different gods. Finally, the Fula of Futa Jalon wanted to control Kaabu so that they could control the trans-Saharan trade routes in that area.

Internally, the Kaabu Empire had become very unstable by the mid-nineteenth century. There were many civil wars within the kingdoms. The Fula took advantage of the situation and made many raids from Futa Jalon. The most important trouble was the war between the King of Sama who refused to hand over the emperorship to Janke Wali Sanneh of Pachana, who was to become the next ruler of the Kaabu Empire. Janke Wali was victorious in the war and became ruler. He started his reign around 1850; and as a new *mansa* (or ruler) making his *dalii* (or prediction), he said that there was going to be a war between the people of Kaabu and those of Futa Jalon which would bring an end to the empire. He therefore called his *tata* or *tato* (fortress) in the capital *turubang* (turubang means total destruction in the Mandinka language). Janke Wali was the last emperor of the empire as it was destroyed in1868.

THE BATTLE OF KANSALA

The war between the people of Kaabu and the Fula was known as the Battle of Kansala. The Fula took fifteen years preparing for this major assault. From Futa Jalon came a confederation of twelve Fula states which included Labe and Timbo. They were also joined by the Fula from Bundu and some discontented Mandinka kings. Their reason for this invasion was that they wanted to convert the people of Kaabu to Islam.

The Fula army consisted of 35,000 to 40,000 men, including 12,000 cavalry. It is believed that the Kaabu army was much inferior to that of their opponents. The people of Kaabu were determined to fight the Fula and protect their empire and traditional religion, even though both their Marabouts and priests of the *jalang* predicted the destruction of the empire.

The Fula army was so big that the son of the reigning emperor, Janke Wali, decided to migrate instead of fighting the invaders. He felt that defeat of the Kaabu army was inevitable. However, the nephew of the emperor and many of the inhabitants decided to fight to death and defend their empire. The Fula first laid siege on the fortress of Kansala for about three months; but being impatient for a breach in the defences, they commenced the battle outside the fortress. The battle raged on for eleven days, with hundreds of Fula killed in the unsuccessful attempt to enter the fortress. The Mandinka defences began to weaken as the days passed. Defeat was inevitable. The Fula finally entered the fortress and a very bloody battle ensued. Thousands died on each side. Many Nyancho women committed suicide by jumping into a well in the fortress rather than become slaves of the Fula. After ensuring that thousands of fighting Fula had entered the fortress, Janke Wali set fire to his seven gunpowder stores. There was an immense explosion, and the fighting stopped immediately. Kansala was completely destroyed. Many believed that it was Janke Wali who ordered that the gates of the fortress be opened to let the invaders in. The destruction of Kansala fulfilled Janke Wali's turubang. Out of the 35,000 or 40,000 men that left Futa Jalon to fight in Kaabu, only 4000 returned home after this fatal battle of 1868.

CONSEQUENCES OF THE WAR

The fall of Kansala brought an abrupt end to the Kaabu Empire, and it never recovered from the fatal blow it received from the Fula. No other Mandinka state was able to rebuild the empire or gain a position of ascendancy. The Fula left a garrison in the Kaabu Region and elected one of their Mandinka allies, the King of Sama, to govern. He attempted to revolt against his Fula overlords, because of the great distance between his province and his overlords but was defeated.

For the first time the Fula of Kaabu realised that the Mandinka were not as invincible as they were made to believe, and as a result one revolt followed another in most Mandinka states. A Fula called Alfa Molloh (or Molloh Egge (or Egue) Baldeh led one such revolt. He succeeded in

14

throwing off Mandinka domination and established a new Fula kingdom for himself, assisted by the Fula of Futa Jalon. He defeated the rulers of Jimara, Tumanna, Kantora, and other states to the south-east and formed what came to be known as the Kingdom of Fulladu. This later developed into an empire. In some states Mandinka rulers were replaced by Fula rulers, although in states like Niani and Sandu the Mandinka were successful in driving out the Fula invaders. (Today, Kaabu is represented by a small province in the eastern part of Guinea-Bissau, where the ruins of Kansala stand as a memorial of what had passed.)

THE SONINKE-MARABOUT WARS

Even before the fall of the Kaabu Empire, Mandinka states on both sides of the River Gambia were faced with the problem of maintaining their political independence, which was threatened by Muslim leaders who wanted to convert the entire population to Islam. For this reason many Mandinka states were unable to go to the assistance of Kaabu, even though they had a joking relationship with her. Since the Mandinka states were determined to maintain their traditional religion, the Muslim leaders who came to be known as marabouts, decided to wage a jihad (or holy war) and convert them by force. These Mandinka who came from the ruling houses of Kaabu and Mali and their subjects were known as Soninke, another word for traditional worshipper. However, the name Soninke is also used for the ethnic group known today as Serahule (Serahuli).

The wars which erupted between the Muslims and the traditional Mandinka worshippers in The Gambia were known as the Soninke-Marabout Wars. The marabouts were invariably Mandinka. Thus, unlike the Kaabu-Futa Jalon War where one ethnic group the Fula fought another, the Mandinka, in The Gambia it was Mandinka fighting Mandinka. Religious difference was one of the main reasons for the wars. But the marabouts, like the Fula, were also dissatisfied with the

15

oppressive rule of the traditional monarchs and wanted to put an end to it. Finally, the marabouts who were traders wanted to control the trade of the river.

The wars started around 1855 and lasted until the latter part of the 1890s, affecting every state in The Gambia Region. However, the various wars did not take place at the same time in every state, and there were times when they were reduced to mere raids and skirmishes. One of the earliest marabouts to wage a war against non-Muslims was Maba Jakhou (Diakhou) Bah, who was greatly influenced by Al-hajj Umar Taal, who in turn had been influenced by such earlier militant Muslims of West Africa as Uthman Dan Fodio, Hamad (or Amadu) of Macina, and Al-Kanemi. Maba Jakhou was mainly interested in spreading Islam, though other followers like Sait Maty, his son; Foday Kombo Sillah, and Foday Kabba Dumbuya added the possibility of carving out kingdoms as well.

During the early years of the jihad, the British were already actively engaged in trade with the local inhabitants, but they were not willing to be involved in local politics because they lacked the funds and the men to enforce their will. At the same time, they had to protect the British traders who were also victims of both Soninke and marabout raids. Thus, once in a while the British were sympathetic to the Soninke and even sent the West Indian Regiment to the village of Sabiji in the Kombo to help.

The wars brought famine and misery and an increase in slavery, which was still practised among the local inhabitants, even though it was no longer recognised by the British. As the wars continued, the original religious reasons were gradually ignored. Marabout leaders competed with one another for political control and tried to build little empires wherever possible. Thus, Muslims fought Muslims and made alliances with non-Muslims. For example, there was a bitter struggle among Maba Jakhou's followers, especially between Biram Ceesay, Sait Maty, Nderi Kani and Mamur Ndari, who was Maba Jakhou's brother. Sometimes Muslim communities were attacked. This meant that many leaders violated the principles of the jihad which forbade attacks on fellow Muslims. One main consequence of the jihad was that many traditional rulers were replaced by marabouts. On the north bank, Niumi, Baddibu, and Jokadu fell to the marabouts. On the south bank, Kombo, Foni, Kantora, Tumanna, and Wuropana all came under Muslim jurisdiction. As some traditional rulers fell from power, there remained a vacuum which many Muslims struggled to fill.

The Soninke-Marabout Wars gave the British the opportunity to colonise The Gambia. Although the earlier policy of the British was non-interference, their attitude changed completely by 1885, when the partition of Africa was well underway and Europeans raced one another to secure colonies in Africa even though these areas were already ruled by African kings and chiefs.

In The Gambia, the British feared that the French would occupy the area where they had traded for over a century. Moreover, they wanted to secure the main waterway (the River Gambia), which they considered to be the best in West Africa. The British, therefore, took advantage of the political instability created by the Soninke-Marabout Wars to gain control of the whole Gambia Region. This changing situation was welcomed by some local inhabitants who were tired of war. But some chiefs and kings like Foday Kombo Sillah and Foday Kabba Dumbuya resented British presence in The Gambia, and resisted the increasing European political control. The British also used the signing of treaties of friendship and commerce with various chiefs to occupy the land of the Mandinka. Examples of these were the rulers of Nianimaru and the Chief of Suara Kunda. In this way, many chiefs signed away their independence. Where they existed, traditional chiefs were maintained to rule but where they were killed by the marabouts the latter replaced them. In the event of a power vacuum or where there were neither Soninke nor marabout chiefs, and where a chief refused to accept the

British, they were deposed by the British and replaced by one of their friends.

The Indirect Rule system was introduced in the various Mandinka states. Chiefs ruled in the name of the sovereign of England. From 1893 and by an ordinance of that year, chiefs were answerable to the Travelling Commissioners, Ozanne on the North Bank and Sitwell on the South Bank respectively. An ordinance of 1902 provided for the protectorate system in the whole country that was further divided into five divisions. Each division had a commissioner who was answerable to the governor at the administrative capital, Bathurst (now Banjul). The divisions were divided into a number of districts and each district was under a head chief called *seefoo* or *seyfu* and assisted by sub-chiefs called *alkalo*. The commissioner was the link between the chiefs and the governor, who was the representative of the sovereign in Britain. The governor appointed and placed a native tribunal in each district. The tribunal looked into certain cases. The chiefs, on behalf of the governor, collected taxes and answered to the demands of the commissioners.

The Mandinka under French rule became part of the French West Africa where the inhabitants were considered as second class citizens. They were outside the Four Communes of St Louis, Gorée, Dakar and Rufisque. In these communes the inhabitants were considered as French citizens. Mandinka chiefs were replaced by other chiefs chosen by the French. Under these chiefs the Mandinka faced many indignities such as flogging and forced labour. It was in these ways that the Mandinka forfeited their independence to the Europeans.

2

THE WOLOF

The Wolof are found mainly in the Senegambia Region, in the area of Walo, Jolof, Kayor (Kajor or Cayor) and parts of Baol and Sine in the Senegal Region. In The Gambia, the Wolof are found in Saloum, north of Niani and in Upper Niumi, Baddibu and Jokadu. The Wolof language can be regarded as the *lingua franca* of the Northern Senegambia Region. This is because it was the language of commerce and communication in the trading centres, especially those frequented by the Moors, Serer, Tukulor, Mandinka, and the many peoples who interacted with them.

ORIGIN AND MIGRATION

The ancestors of the Wolof are believed to have migrated from the Sahara Desert area. They were one of the earlier peoples who inhabited this now hostile region, before it became a desert. As the once fertile land gradually dried up, the people began to move in different directions in search of environments that were more conducive to human habitation and agriculture.

According to tradition, the ancestors of the Wolof, during this period of forced migration, gradually moved into the area north of Senegal that became known as Futa Toro and Mauritania.

Between 639 and 642 AD, the Arabs conquered Egypt first, and then the rest of North Africa. They gradually forced the Berbers who originally lived in the area to move south, thus causing further southward migration. At about the same time, the Fula moved from the east into Futa Toro. The ancestors of the Wolof were, in turn, forced to move from Mauritania and Futa Toro into northern and eastern Senegal. As they moved, they forced the few Serer and Mandinka who had earlier settled in the area to move into Sine, Saloum, and the Upper

19

Gambia regions. The Wolof then settled in small villages under chiefs or lamans, each independent of the other. It is believed that the villages gradually developed into states and kingdoms. One such kingdom was Jolof, which was later conquered in the mid-thirteenth century by the generals of Sundiata Keita, the Mandinka emperor of ancient Mali. By the fourteenth century, Jolof was no longer a vassal of Mali because it, too, had formed its own empire.

THE JOLOF EMPIRE

The Wolof called their empire Jolof. It comprised the kingdoms or states of Jolof which served as an overlord controlling Walo, Kayor, and Baol on the coast, Sine and Saloum, Serer states in the south, and finally Dimar, which was an inland state east of Walo. It was believed that this empire was formed either by voluntary association or by conquest. By voluntary association, we mean that all these states willingly agreed to form a single political entity - an empire - and accepted Jolof as their overlord. Since it is unlikely that people or states would willingly give up their independence it can be assumed that member states agreed to form an empire because they were threatened by other powerful neighbours and felt more secure in a bigger entity; or that the kingdom of Jolof was powerful enough to conquer the surrounding states. But even though these states were tribute-paying vassals, they maintained a great deal of independence, especially in political affairs. They sometimes contributed contingents to the army of Jolof and paid such tributes as salt, fish, cattle and grass for thatching the roofs of huts. The weak control exercised by Jolof over her vassals was confirmed by the early Portuguese explorers and traders.

As more and more Europeans traded with such coastal states as Kayor, Walo, and Baol, they became powerful enough to challenge the authority of their overlord. It was their fight for political independence that led to the final disintegration of this empire in 1560. Kayor set the example by rebelling and gaining her independence. All the other vassal states followed her example. After this, Jolof tried very hard to rebuild the empire but she failed because the former vassal states were determined to maintain their newly earned freedom. None of the former vassal states was able to build an empire in Jolof's place, although in

20

some instances, Kayor was able to absorb Baol and set up dual rulership. Each Wolof state was constantly occupied by its own internal problems and, at the same time, sought to maintain its independence from its neighbours. But with the increased presence of the Europeans, they had a new problem to contend with, and this was to keep the Europeans out of their internal political affairs.

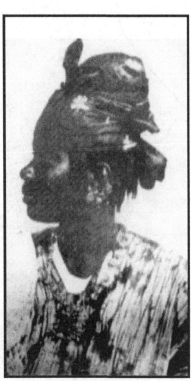

Fig 3. A Wolof man   Fig 4. A Wolof woman

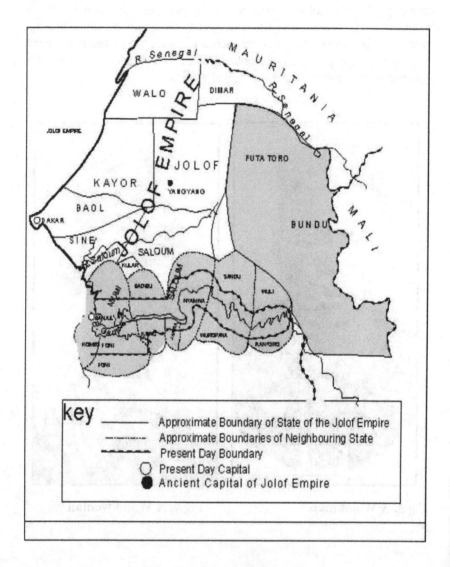

Map 4 - The Jolof Empire

DEVELOPMENT OF THE JOLOF EMPIRE

Although the actual date of the origin of the Wolof states remains obscure, Walo was said to be in existence by the end of the eleventh century. In fact, it is believed to be the first state and therefore the cradle of Wolof development. Walo started as a small Serer settlement headed by a laman. By the tenth century, it was under a lineage of the Ja-ogo dynasty.

The history of Walo is linked to that of ancient Ghana, the first empire of the Western Sudan, which was destroyed by the Almoravids in 1076. These Almoravids were Berbers who launched a jihad in order to convert the whole population of Ghana and to regain their trading centre, Awdagost. This had been captured earlier by the people of the Ghana Empire. The leader of this movement in Western Sudan was Abu Bakr Ibn Muhamed, who succeeded in destroying Ghana. However, he did not rebuild the empire but settled in the region and married a woman called Fatimata Sal. Abu Bakr was never accepted by the local inhabitants and was therefore faced with constant rebellions. He was seriously wounded in 1087 while trying to suppress a rebellion. He then left the area to seek treatment, but died soon after his departure.

LEGEND OF NJANJAN NJIE

Njanjan Njie is believed to be the first ruler of Walo and founder of the empire of Jolof. According to tradition, he was the son of Abu Bakr Ibn Muhamed and Fatimata Sal. He was called Amadu Bubakar Ibn Muhamed. A few years after the death of his father, his mother, Fatimata Sal, remarried her husband's former slave, and Amadu Bubakar threw himself into the strong currents of the river as a sign of his total rejection of the marriage. Many believed him to be dead, but he survived because he was a good swimmer. He lived an almost amphibious life, hiding by the banks of the River Senegal.

Legend has it that he eventually emerged from hiding because he wanted to prevent bloodshed among a group of fishermen of Mengen who were quarrelling over the distribution of firewood. The villagers were astonished by his appearance and thought that he was a genii or spirit from the river.

23

He further surprised them when he shared the firewood fairly and thus prevented bloodshed. He then disappeared, much to their dismay. The villagers decided to capture him, so they pretended to have another quarrel. When he appeared again to mediate, they captured him. He refused to communicate with them, but his silence was broken by a beautiful woman who talked to him. She was later given to him in marriage.

In the meantime, the elders of the village had sent a delegation to a seer and diviner in the neighbouring state of Sine, who was also the ruler. He was called Mansa Wali Jon. On hearing this story, the King of Sine exclaimed "Njanjan Njie", which in his native Serer language means "This is extra-ordinary". The delegation from the fishing village, on hearing this, concluded that it was the name of the stranger. From that time, Amadu Bubakar became known as Njanjan Njie. Mansa Wali Jon assured the people that the stranger was not a genii but that every state in the area should accept him as their overlord. He was the first to pledge his allegiance to Njanjan Njie. All the other leaders of the surrounding states followed his example. It was for this reason that people believed that the empire was formed by voluntary association.

Njanjan Njie returned to Walo and became the first ruler of the state. After governing for about sixteen years, he decided to go into self-exile because of the growing dissatisfaction over his reign. He went to the state of Jolof. Here he impressed the local chief with his dignity and intelligence, and he was made ruler of that state. His brother, by his mother's second marriage, Barka Mbody Wade, continued to rule in Walo.

WOLOF KINGDOMS

There were four typical Wolof kingdoms during and after the existence of the Jolof Empire. These were Jolof, Kayor, Walo, and Baol. The Fula, Serer, Mandinka, Moors and other ethnic groups formed the minority within each Wolof state. Each of these ethnic groups had its own spokesman in the king's government. Kingship belonged to specific matrilineages or, as in the case of Jolof, patrilineages. The most influential candidates among the various royal houses, 'neeg' in the Wolof language or royal lineages were usually chosen as kings.

After the disintegration of the Jolof Empire, there were frequent internal and inter-state wars which came about as a result of rivalry among the lineages. This led to a great deal of political instability. There were also frequent assassinations of kings and sometimes of their entire families to ensure that lineages would be unable to present future candidates for the throne. In a struggle between two royal lineages in Walo around 1735, for example, the entire family of the ruler, Yerim Mbanyik Anta Jobe (Diop), was put to death by his opponent. In another incident another ruler of Walo was killed on the day of his coronation. There were also many inter-state wars. In 1733, a bitter war occurred between Kayor and Walo as a result of a family quarrel. The ruler of Walo had refused to return the belongings of his wife, the mother of the ruler of Kayor, after she had left him. This war lasted for several months. The frequency of these internecine wars helped neighbouring states, like Mauritania, Futa Toro, and even the other Wolof states, to take advantage of the periods of instability and to interfere in the politics of whichever state was affected.

However, there were also many alliances which were further strengthened by marriages. These agreements of friendship did not necessarily prevent wars, as the Walo-Kayor war showed. But there were times when alliances helped to maintain peace. During wars the peasant population suffered most because they were often raided and enslaved by the army of their respective kings and nobles and by the armies of states or groups who were taking the offensive. To escape this difficult position, many peasants either joined the armies or joined marabout clerics who were rarely bothered by such wars.

The arrival of, first, the Portuguese and, later, other Europeans added a new dimension to the struggles for supremacy. The ruler of Jolof gradually lost his grip on the vassal states, especially the three coastal states of Kayor, Walo, and Baol, which became rich from their trade with the Europeans. Jolof was an inland state and could not derive full benefit from the Atlantic trade. Jolof's position was made worse by the invasion of the Fula from Futa Toro led by Koli Tengella, a new leader of the state. With these disadvantages, it was no surprise that the vassal states became free. Kayor's revolt was led by Amari Ngone Sobel who also became the first ruler of the independent state of Kayor. Attempts by Jolof at reconquering Kayor only resulted in the death of the reigning ruler of Jolof, Leeli Fuli Fak.

The struggle among the Wolof states continued. Kayor became the most powerful and succeeded in conquering Baol. The King of Kayor, Latir Sukaabe Faal (1697 – 1719), became the ruler of both Kayor and Baol. This practice of dual kingship was enjoyed by eight kings of Kayor, though these states were sometimes ruled by two separate kings. In 1759, however, Birayamb Ma-Dyigen (Jigen) Ndaw Njie defeated and exiled the reigning ruler of Kayor, Ma Isa Bige Ngone. But his victory was short-lived because in the following year the exiled ruler of Kayor returned and killed the King of Jolof in 1760. Ma Isa died three years later after regaining his throne.

These types of political quarrels and power struggles continued to the end of the nineteenth century and prevented any kind of united front against common enemies. In fact, the instability favoured the rise of Futa Toro in the early 1600s, and by 1638 all the kingdoms north of the Senegambia Region were paying tribute to Futa Toro, though they were able to regain their freedom by the 1660s. By 1673, the Wolof states were faced with a new threat. The Muslims from Mauritania waged a jihad across the north of Senegal. The war lasted till 1677, and every Wolof state fell to the Muslims. At this time the vast majority of the Wolof population still adhered to the traditional religions. The Muslim invaders were nicknamed toubanan (from the Wolof word toub, which means to convert). All the Wolof states and Futa Toro, which also suffered from the invasion, were then ruled by Muslims who came to be known as *buur jullit* (Muslim ruler).

The movement was a threat both to the Wolof states and to the French traders in St. Louis. The French therefore allied with the Wolof and helped them regain their freedom from the Moors. Incessant raids and long periods of famine, which brought the Kingdom of Walo closer to the French, followed the wars. The French played an active part in the defeat of the marabouts. From this period onwards, the Wolof states became more concerned about their struggle for political independence from the French, who were then taking a more active part in the politics of the people than about the growing influence of the marabouts.

EFFECTS OF THE MARABOUT WARS

One major result of the marabout wars in the north of Senegal was the creation of two powerful emirates, the Brakna and the Trarza, in Mauritania. This was to have severe repercussions on the gum trade that had developed with European presence. The emirates continued to be a constant threat both to the Wolof states and to the French during and after the development of the gum trade, which became an important part of the Atlantic trade during this period. The emirates' threat continued well into the end of the eighteenth century, and so many people were taken prisoner in the wars and enslaved that the French feared the source of slaves would dry up and so put a premature end to the slave trade.

The ease with which the people of the Wolof states were captured led to a situation whereby the French joked about it, by saying that the Moors had promised the people of the Wolof states that they would show them how to get coos or millet without any cultivation. This was rather ironic because the inhabitants of these states did not have any millet at all because of the constant raids carried out by the Moors, the Fula, and the soldiers of the kings and nobles. These attackers took the foodstuffs and eventually, the peasants found it practically impossible to cultivate the land. The months and years of starvation that followed led many people into voluntary slavery. Moreover, the cravings of the traditional rulers and the nobles for European goods encouraged them to sell their people into slavery. As was expected, the defeat of the marabouts led to further expansion of French trade, which in turn meant further penetration into the interior of Senegal. The most noticeable effect was a further extension of French influence into more areas of the Wolof states.

Like the Mandinka, the Wolof had stratified social and political structures. The nobility was at the top of the political and social ladder.

The peasants (called *baadoola*), cultivated the land and produced the millet or coos that was their staple food. Cultivation of millet was done on communal, family and personal levels. Millet was so important that women and young men, who were preparing for marriage, were given their own plot to cultivate. Some women handed over their land to their husbands or male relatives to cultivate and the proceeds were handed to them. They did what they liked with their millet harvests though they invariably used it to supplement the meals that were provided for the family. For the farmers, it was necessary to have enough millet to cover the year's meals especially the dry season. They therefore hoarded the millet and other foodstuffs. This sometimes resulted in members of the nobility raiding the peasants because they knew that they always had surpluses. Groundnuts were given much importance after its introduction as a cash crop. The money derived from its sale provided the cash needed to buy more millet and other basic necessities such as clothes, farming implements and sometimes cows which in turn were used for such celebrations as male circumcision, marriages and festivals. The Wolof also kept goats, sheep and chickens.

Cotton was grown and weavers produced the cloths of the inhabitants. Cloths imported by the Europeans later supplemented these. Equally important was the production of indigo that was used to dye the clothes worn. The colours were blue or black.

Palm oil was purchased locally and used for cooking and medicinal purposes but the Europeans later became the main purchasers. The palm juice from the palm tree that became palm wine when fermented was a popular beverage among the Wolof.

Like the Mandinka artisans, the Wolof artisans also had their own black and goldsmiths, weavers, leather workers and woodcarvers. The griots among the Wolof also kept the histories of the states and families and passed the knowledge from one generation to the other.

When resident near the sea or river the Wolof had fishermen who provided fish for the population. Like the other ethnic groups, they also had hunters. However, trading was dominated by Serahule and Mandinka traders, although the Wolof eventually produced a handful in Bathurst (Banjul) and a few other places in The Gambia and the major cities and towns of Senegal.

END OF WOLOF INDEPENDENCE

The Kingdom of Walo was the first Wolof state to be ruled by the French. As always, Walo was faced with a bitterly disputed succession, and at the critical time in the early part of the nineteenth century there was a hotly disputed one. From this time Walo became the victim of the Moors, the Tukulor, and the French. The first two groups of people were again engaged in raids. The king's niece, Njombot, who had helped him to become ruler, by presenting him as a candidate, married the leader of the Trarza Moors in 1833. This move alarmed the French because they knew that the reigning King of Walo was weak and that power was really in the hands of the princess Njombot, who in turn was controlled by her husband. By this time, the king's soldiers (the *cheddo* of Walo) were even more difficult to control because they had better access to guns and ammunition.

The ruler of Walo had become so poor that he had to sell one of his villages to the French for a mere 700 francs. At the same time, he appealed to the French to help him save the rest of his state. But the people were so divided that everyone knew that the downfall of the state was inevitable. The impoverished old ruler died a blind and disappointed man. His death occasioned another power struggle for control of the throne, and again Princess Njombot succeeded in having her cousin, Mbody Malek, elected ruler. She managed to retain her power and influence, much to the disappointment of the French. In any case, her cousin, the reigning king, was as weak as his predecessor. For the next fifteen years of his reign, power really remained in the hands of the princess until she died in 1846. Then the princess' younger sister, Ndate Yalla, seized power with the help of the French who hoped to manipulate her and thereby realise their dreams of gaining control over the state.

The queen, Ndate Yalla, soon proved to be formidable and a year later the French, much to their discomfort, became aware of the fact that she would not become their puppet. She was soon criticising the French for their interference in the internal politics of the state and for refusing to pay the customary taxes. She had the strong support of her husband, who was a member of the nobility from the state of Kayor. The French resented the queen's criticism, for they felt it was their duty to protect

29

the people in their sphere of influence from the Moors who were still harassing them after the death of Njombot.

Thus, the people of Walo were caught in the rivalry between the French and the Moors. Whenever they were more inclined to favour the French, they were raided by the Moors, and when they showed any sign of friendship towards the Moors, they were punished by the French.

By 1859, the French persisted in refusing to pay the usual customary tax on the excuse that the company of French merchants in St. Louis was constantly pillaged by the inhabitants of Walo. This did not help to improve relations. The struggle for power in the state of Walo became a three-cornered fight between the supporters of the deposed ruler, the husband of the reigning queen, who wanted to make sure that their son would become ruler after his wife's death, and the people who felt that the real ruler should be the son of the deceased Princess Njombot. This last group was also supported by the Moors.

It was in the middle of this political tension that the Frenchman Faidherbe was sent as Governor of the French coastal settlements with his headquarters at St. Louis in Senegal in 1854. He was an ardent imperialist and was determined to embark on territorial expansion. He insisted that the river Senegal belonged to the French and, therefore, his main objective was to rid the river states of the influence of the Moors and the state of Walo. For the first time, the Moors and the people of Walo saw the French as a common enemy, and even though their combined forces were defeated by the French in 1855, they did not ease up their opposition to European presence. Faidherbe burnt down villages in Walo and obtained much booty: cattle, horses, sheep, donkeys and a few camels. He also took one hundred and fifty prisoners of war that included members of the nobility.

The queen, Ndate Yalla, the last *linger* of Walo, went into exile in the neighbouring state of Kayor. The ruler, who had been deposed earlier by the queen, put up a short resistance with the help of some of the chiefs. He was defeated by the French and, unable to withstand the shame of this defeat, went into exile in Futa Toro with some of his supporters. Many of the villages in Walo were deserted, and the French gained full control of the state.

Faidherbe placed a governor in the state that was regarded as the supreme chief of the region. Walo was divided into four districts each headed by a local chief responsible to the French. For many years, the Moors and cheddo from Walo continued to oppose Faidherbe. The state then became the base for further French expansion into the rest of Senegal and Western Sudan. The French did not immediately follow their success and capture the rest of the Wolof states because they felt they should only put an end to Moorish domination and control the trade of the river Senegal. Before Faidherbe could complete this task, he was recalled to France in 1865. His successors were not, at this time, as ambitious as he was and were further constrained by cut-backs in their expansion of activities. By the latter part of the 1880 their docile policy had changed, for the French were determined to control the whole of Senegal.

The French interfered in the internal politics of the rest of the Wolof states. Lat Jor Jobe (Diop), the ruler of Kayor who had been deposed by the French as ruler, but reinstated in 1871 waged many wars against Baol and eventually became the ruler. He was however killed in a battle with the French on 27 October 1886. His death brought the states of Baol and Kayor under French rule. The French then turned to Alburi Njie, the ruler of the Jolof State. He was first forced into exile in May 1890 and was far from his state when he was eventually killed in a war with the French in 1901.

The Wolof of The Gambia in places like Niumi, Jokadu, Sabach and Sandial were brought under the Indirect Rule system that the British imposed on the peoples. Like the Mandinka their head chiefs collected taxes for the governor at Bathurst and obeyed the directives of the commissioners. Thus like people in other parts of Africa, the Wolof people lost their independence to the Europeans.

3

THE SERER

The Serer are also referred to as Serere in The Gambia. Today, they live in great numbers in the former states of Sine, Saloum and among the Mandinka of Jokadu and Niumi in the Senegambia Region. Serer are also found in large numbers in the areas of the former kingdoms of Baol, Kayor, and Jolof. The Serer are sometimes sub-divided into Serer-Sine, Serer-Nones, Serer-N'doute, and Serer-Njenghen or Safen. The first group, the Serer-Sine, occupy the Sine and Saloum areas of the Senegambia Region and parts of Niumi and Baddibu in The Gambia; the second, Serer-Nones, in the Thies area of Senegal; the third, the Serer-N'doute, in southern Kayor; and the fourth Serer-Njenghen or Safen are located in Baol. Each group speaks a different dialect of the Serer language.

THE MIGRATION OF THE SERER AND FOUNDING OF SERER STATES

The most popular belief is that the Serer migrated from Kaabu in the Upper Casamance about four hundred years ago. This migration was caused by a civil war after the death of one of the kings. War broke out between the dead king's brother and his son, Boure, for control of the throne. Boure was defeated and left the state with his supporters. They moved northwards passing through Foni, then across the River Gambia to Baddibu, and eventually founded their first settlement, Mbissel, near Juwaala (Joal) in the area that later made up the state of Sine. Another tradition claims that the Serer settlements were later ruled by Mandinka Nyanchos who migrated from Kaabu.

During the Serer migration, they met small groups of Mandinka, whom they either incorporated into their society or defeated in battle. The Serer decided to settle in forest areas because the environment proved favourable to their culture. Chiefs who had the local name *laman* ruled the first settlements. Consequently, many Serer settled in the Wolof and northern Gambian states where they established towns and villages.

One group of migrant Mandinka intermingled with the Serer and eventually controlled them, but assimilated Serer culture and language. These Mandinka rulers came to be known as *gelwar* (or *guelewar*), in the states of Sine and Saloum. They were Nyanchos (a branch of the ruling class of Kaabu). The first gelwar ruler in Sine was known as Mansa Wali Jon with his capital at Jakhao (Diakhao). The system of inheritance was matrilineal, as was the case in Kaabu. Thus, when Mansa Wali died, his sister's son succeeded him. This royal lineage was established in Sine by the end of the fourteenth century.

Saloum, the other Serer state, was ruled by a grand-nephew of Mansa Wali Jon. He was called M'began N'dure. However, his position of kingship was gained through conquest rather than by inheritance. He waged a successful war against the marabouts that were in control of Saloum at the latter part of the fourteenth century. He built a new capital called Kahone (Kawoon). The gelwar kings took the title *buur* and ruled Sine and Saloum well into the nineteenth century, when the French conquered them. In their earlier stages, both Sine and Saloum were vassal states of the King of Jolof, by either voluntary association or conquest. However, it was considered to be voluntary because, according to tradition, Mansa Wali Jon had proposed the acceptance of Jolof authority. By the mid-sixteenth century Sine, Saloum and other vassal states had gained their independence, especially when Kayor rebelled against the political domination of the state of Jolof.

Sine and Saloum later extended their boundaries to a great extent, encompassing parts of the Wolof states of Baol and Kayor in Senegal and the Mandinka state of Niumi in The Gambia. These states paid tribute to the rulers of the Serer states. Furthermore some Serer settled among the Mandinka of Jokadu, the Wolof in the areas of Sabach and Sandial in The Gambia and the Jolof state in Northern Senegal.

Rulers of the Serer states of Sine and Saloum formed marriage alliances with kings, princes, and princesses of neighbouring states in order to encourage peace and further migration of people thereby expanding Serer areas of settlement. One such alliance was the marriage between the ruler of Kayor, Birayma Faatim-Penda, and a gelwar woman from the state of Saloum called Kodu Joof. This marriage enabled their son to have claims to both the thrones of Kayor and Saloum through the female line. However, like the Wolof states, the Serer states were almost always engaged in disputed successions, as there were many claimants to the thrones. This led to political instability and civil strife causing many to migrate to more peaceful areas.

Wars with neighbouring states and peoples forced many Serer to migrate to other areas. The Soninke-Marabout wars initiated by Maba Jakhu Bah in the early 1860s, for example, against the people of Sine and Saloum caused the migration of over 2000 Serer from Sine, Saloum and Baddibu where some had earlier settled. From Essau to Sabach, the land was left desolate with much loss of life as a result of these wars. Numerous towns were burnt down. Practically destitute, the Serer fled to Barra to seek British protection. Many were given permission to cross the river and settle in Kombo. A few settled in Bathurst in the area known as Half Die. A smaller number of the Serer was used for the building of the road to the place called Oyster Creek in Bathurst. Maba also attacked the French in Kaolack thereby causing further migration from Saloum to The Gambia. The refugees that migrated to Bathurst and Kombo also included a few Christian Serer. The Portuguese had introduced Christianity in Senegal but it did not have a firm base. The French Catholic missionaries reintroduced it in 1779. However, it was not until the 1840s that French missionaries went into the Sine and Saloum areas and were successful in converting a handful of Serer to the Catholic religion.

The Serer migrants, like the inhabitants of Sine and Saloum, engaged in farming and cultivated especially *coos* (or millet) and corn. It was from coos flour that *cherreh*, a popular Serer cereal. was prepared by their women. The flour was made into fine small balls, the size of grains of sand and steamed in clay colanders. The cherreh was and is still the favourite food of the Serer.

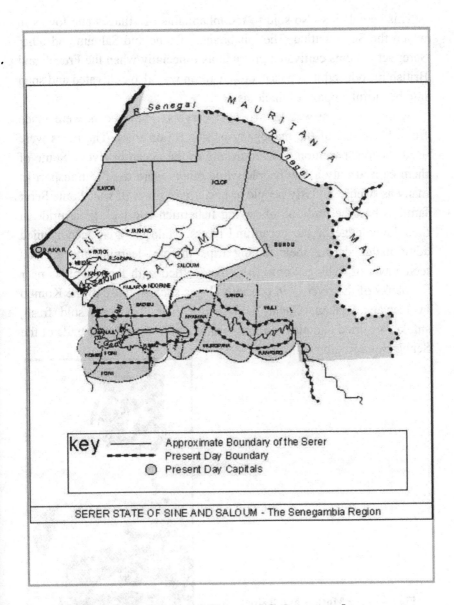

SERER STATE OF SINE AND SALOUM - The Senegambia Region

Map 5 - The Serer States of Sine and Saloum and Neighbouring States

This cereal was also sold to the inhabitants of villages and towns in which the Serer settled. The inhabitants of Sine and Saloum and other Serer settlements cultivated groundnuts especially when the French and British introduced it as a cash crop. Cotton was also cultivated and spun into beautiful lappas or loincloths.

Serer men were well-known boat carvers. These boats were made from the trunks of the mahogany or silk cotton trees. The boats were used for transportation and for fishing in the ocean or rivers. Some of them carried only a few people while others were used to transport as many as twenty to thirty people, especially in times of war. Some Serer families had the tradition of having fishermen and took great pride in their knowledge of the ocean and rivers. Male children accompanied adult males during their fishing trips thereby learning the art and techniques of fishing. Some fishermen settled with their families near the banks of the river or in coastal villages such as those of the Kombo in Jeswang, Bakau, Gunjur and Brufut. The fish were sold fresh, smoked or dried and played an important part in the internal trade of the Senegambia Region.

Fig 5 - Serer Mother and Baby

Since Sine and Saloum have large salt deposits, Serer men and sometimes women traded this commodity in villages, towns and states where it was not available. During the colonial period, the inhabitants of Bathurst bought some of their salt from the Serer. The salt was transported in baskets or jute bags. Salt was also exchanged for European goods such as beads, knives and cloth.

Serer men were the main suppliers of firewood that was collected from the mangrove swamps. They sold firewood to the inhabitants of Bathurst, which included Wolof, Mandinka, Fula, Creole and Aku. As with the royal lineage of Sine and Saloum, the Serer in general practised the matrilineal system of inheritance and family and lineage ties were very strong. Some of the lineages included the Joof, Faye, Sarr, Mboge and Ndure.

THE FRENCH, SONINKE-MARABOUT WARS AND THE END OF SERER INDEPENDENCE

The nineteenth century ushered in a change of fortune for the Serer states. Although there were many French traders and missionaries in Sine and Saloum, these states were only of secondary importance to the French administrators at Gorée and St. Louis. By 1859, there was an inevitable confrontation which led to the gradual occupation of the Sine-Saloum area by the French. The jihads in Sine and Saloum led by Maba Jakhou Bah and other marabouts facilitated French interference in the politics of the two states.

In addition, French traders and missionaries made constant complaints about the raids of the people of Sine and Saloum. Though some of the accusations were false, they provided the French with the opportunity to invade the Serer states. One such invasion was led by the Governor of St. Louis and Gorée Louis Faidherbe, whose real aim was to nullify the earlier treaties signed by the rulers of these states, so that they could sign new ones that would be to the advantage of the French merchants. He first attacked Sine and either captured or killed over one hundred and fifty fighters. The ruler of Saloum, Samba Laobe Faal, was at this time engaged in a struggle for the throne with his father, Ma Kodu Joof, and did not take the offensive against the French because an earlier defeat of Sine was an eye-opener for him. The rulers of both the states of Sine and Saloum distrusted each other and failed to create a united force against the French. In 1861, the French administrators forced the reigning rulers of Saloum, Samba Laobe Faal and Sine, Kumba Ndoffen Ndure to sign treaties with them and were able to lay down the terms because of their military superiority over these rulers.

The following year, the ruler of Sine began to react against the French by causing trouble among the traders in his state so as to force further French concessions. He forbade his subjects to cultivate groundnuts, since he believed that the French would leave his state if they had no groundnuts to buy. But these laws affected the local inhabitants because they had come to depend on groundnuts to exchange for European goods. In Saloum, the ruler continued to resist the French. He was then attacked in 1862 but they failed to compromise with him. The French took about four hundred and fifty prisoners as a punitive measure against further resistance.

Each encounter with the Europeans placed the rulers of these states at a disadvantageous position. Luckily for them, the French at this time were only interested in trade and not in effective occupation. The Serer leaders believed that the only way to maintain their independence and prevent permanent European settlement was to stop the missionaries and traders from constructing permanent buildings. This rule was maintained by all the rulers even though some of their treaties with the French included a clause that they should be allowed to build in stone. As far as the Serer kings were concerned, the inclusion of this clause was just a means of keeping the French temporarily satisfied. These disturbances caused more Serer to move to The Gambia. They included a handful of Serer who had become Christians as a result of missionary activities from the 1840s onwards.

The need for the Serer kings to maintain their independence remained very important and they sought help even from the French who were formerly considered their enemies. Thus, when the marabouts from Baddibu, led by the well-known Maba Jakhou Bah, threatened their independence in the 1860s, the King of Sine turned to the French for help, even though he did not trust them. Both Sine and Saloum were strongly attached to the traditional religion. Thus, it was not a surprise that the marabouts were determined to convert them. The French did not offer the expected help, but both states fought bitterly to maintain their political independence.

In Saloum, Maba was not only fighting a jihad, but was also involved in a disputed succession between Samba Laobe Faal, the King of Saloum, and his father, Ma Kodu Joof, who had earlier rejected the throne of Saloum for that of Kayor. But his reign in Kayor was short. His refusal to co-operate with the French in the building of a telegraph led to his deposition and exile in 1861. He, therefore, claimed the throne of Saloum but his son was unwilling to relinquish power. As a result, civil war erupted. Ma Kodu had been converted to Islam by Maba, who agreed to help him gain the throne. Over two hundred and fifty people were killed in the civil war but Maba was unable to get the throne for Ma Kodu, who died in 1863 a rather disappointed man.

The marabouts' encounter with Sine was rather tragic for them. It was during this time that Maba was killed at the Battle of Somb in 1867. The gunpowder of the marabouts was wet, making defeat inevitable. For many years, the King of Sine boasted of this victory, which for some time ensured the independence of the Serer state from the marabouts. A large area of Sine and Saloum was devastated as a result of the wars, and thousands of people either fled or were killed. The Serer rulers were later able to rebuild the areas because the followers of Maba were for many years engaged in internal disputes for the leadership.

Unfortunately, both Sine and Saloum were also engaged in disputed succession and civil wars, which resulted in political instability. In Sine, for example, five rulers ruled in five years. The French took advantage of this internal strife to get more and more concessions from whoever ruled. They usually promised to give the rulers arms and ammunition even though the French had no intention of keeping their side of the bargain. By the latter part of the nineteenth century, the French were interested in effective occupation and control over the chiefs. In 1884, for example, the governor signed a treaty with the King of Sine to grant the French traders permission to build in stone. In return, they were to give him aid in the form of arms and ammunition. But this promised aid never reached the king, for the French were not prepared to supply weapons to someone who might later turn against them.

In Baddibu, the marabouts continued to fight for supremacy. They made strange alliances, for example, Mamur Ndari, the brother of Maba, allied with his former enemy, Biram Ceesay, and the non-Muslim ruler of Saloum, called Guedel Mboge (M'bodj), to fight against Maba's son, Sait Maty. After suffering many defeats, Sait Maty retaliated by attacking Saloum. The French claimed that the attack was directed against them and sent a column of soldiers to Kahone, the capital of Saloum. The French defeated the marabout forces and forced Sait Maty to seek refuge with the British in The Gambia. The French demanded the return of Sait Maty, but since the British refused to hand him over, he stayed in the village of Bakau near Bathurst (Banjul) until his death in 1897.

After the defeat and exile of Sait Maty, the French hoisted their flag in the marabout state of Baddibu, while other marabout leaders and the King of Saloum looked on. They then signed a treaty with the French which was aimed, according to the French administrator, at putting an end to the wars in the whole area and at bringing prosperity to everyone.

However, by this treaty, the African leaders basically acknowledged a French protectorate over Nioro, the marabout capital, and the rest of French Baddibu. Those who objected to the treaty were deported to Gabon, a French possession down the coast of West Africa. The establishment of a French protectorate in the area was greatly resented by the British, who felt that the French had annexed an area that they would have liked for themselves. Consequently, the British and French were engaged in bitter arguments that were finally settled when both European powers signed treaties in 1889, settling the various boundary disputes.

The French needed to hold on to Sine and Saloum because the groundnut trade was improving with the years. They took the civil wars as an excuse to interfere. In 1891, they invited both the King of Saloum, Guedel Mboge, and the King of Sine, M'bake Deb Njie, to St. Louis to sign treaties with the governor. By the treaties, they agreed to make their states protectorates of France, and also to give the French land on which they would build military posts, roads, railways or anything else that would help promote their commercial interests. In return, the French agreed that the thrones of Sine and Saloum would remain hereditary to the children of the two rulers. Sine and Saloum were divided into districts like the other areas where the French had seized political control. The French maintained their control over who would be the chiefs of the states, districts, and villages. Local inhabitants who opposed the treaties were arrested by the French and deported to other French territories in West Africa. Thus, the people of Sine and Saloum lost their political independence.

4

THE FULA

The Fula, or Peul as they are known by some people in the Senegambia Region, are widely dispersed in West Africa. They are also known in other countries by other names, such as Fulbe and Fulani. Today they are found in every modern West African state from Mauritania to Cameroon, and the Republic of the Sudan. In such countries as Sierra Leone, Liberia, and Mauritania they form one of the minority groups.

ORIGIN AND MIGRATION

There are numerous and often improbable claims about the origin of the Fula, most of whom are light-skinned in colour and of slender build. Historians, ethnologists, and the Fula themselves (oral historians) claim that the ancestors of the Fula were whites who had migrated into Africa. Thus, it has been claimed that their ancestors were Semites, Europeans (Britons and Romans), Cushites (Ethiopians and Egyptians) and Berbers. These claims have been corroborated by the light complexion, silky hair and straight noses of many Fula compared to the black or brown complexion, kinky hair and flat noses of other ethnic groups of the region such as the Jola, Mandinka and Wolof. But of all these claims, the Semitic is the most popular one. In any case, it is almost certain that the ancestors of the Fula migrated from outside the African continent.

Futa Toro, in the northeast of Senegal, is the cradle of the Fula in Africa, as this area is believed to be their original home. The Fula, being mainly cattle herders, are mostly nomadic people, and their dispersal from Futa Toro has been attributed to over-population and the search for better grazing ground for their cattle. Sometimes the Fula migrants formed new settlements which later developed into states. The most important of these states formed outside Senegambia were Macina and Futa Jalon in Guinea. Futa Bundu in Eastern Senegal was a Tukulor state founded in the seventeenth century, but it also had and still has a very large number of Fula settlers. There are four main groups of Fula in the region. These are the Fula (Peul) Futa from Futa Toro, Fula (Peul) Bundu from the state of Bundu, Fula (Peul) Futa Jalon from Futa Jalon in Guinea and Fula (Peul) Firdu who came from the state of Firdu in the Kaabu Empire. Whereas the Fula of Futa Toro and Futa Bundu were based in Senegal and had migrated from their homeland to The Gambia, those of Futa Jalon and Firdu migrated from Guinea and Firdu respectively.

The Fula were invariably cattle herders who migrated from place to place in search of fertile land for the grazing of their animals. As they migrated, they sometimes settled on the land of the Mandinka and Wolof with an agreement to pay certain taxes to the rulers. They even looked after the cattle of their landlords, though some landowners overtaxed and maltreated them. In a sense they could be considered as not being subject to any kings of the country and although they lived in their territory, they usually moved out or broke up when they were overburdened by the misbehaviour of their overlords. They also moved out when the soil was no longer fertile. Thus the Fula did not build mud huts like the Mandinka or Wolof but instead built circular cane huts with the use of grass, corn or coos sticks and sometimes covered the walls and floors with cow dung. These cane huts were easily abandoned or destroyed enabling them to move on.

The life of the herders was very difficult. They walked long distances looking for good areas to graze their animals. At night they constantly watched out for thieves and other wild animals like lions. They lit fires round the cattle to keep awake. In The Gambia, cattle herders moved to higher ground from the riverbanks during the rainy season but moved back to the banks during the dry season. Here, they were on constant watch for crocodiles that would attack the cattle, especially the young. Despite these difficulties many Fula continued to engage in cattle breeding. Their wealth was measured by the size of their herds, which ranged from fifty to one hundred and twenty head and sometimes much more per family. Even today, the wealth of a typical Fula is measured by the number of cattle he owns. The Fula were always reluctant to kill their cattle for local consumption as they felt that this would minimise their wealth and because their Mandinka rulers usually demanded a share of the meat. Thus these animals were killed only for the funerals of certain individuals, that of their leader, for example. Their affection for their cattle was a guiding principle in their lives. Their women usually exchanged fresh milk, sour milk and butter for beads, knives, salt and other trifling with their neighbours and even the Europeans. Women plaited beads and coins in their tresses. The Fula also ate some of the butter and used some on their bodies and hair.

Fig 6 - A Young Fula Girl

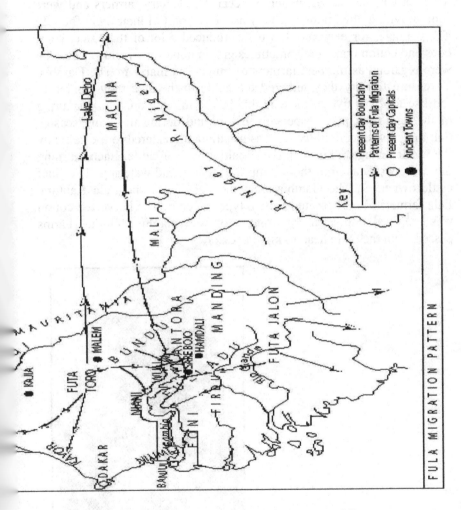

Map 6 - The Patterns of Fula Migration - Settlements and States

While e migratory trend is true for a large number of Fula, the situation changed gradually for many, during the process of migration and political development. As they moved from state to state, certain Fula either completely gave up their nomadic life or became semi-nomadic, moving periodically, for example, for every five or more years. Some of the Fula who settled permanently became sedentary farmers and were soon providing the grains that they needed as part of their daily food. In The Gambia, for example, the Fula produced a lot of their rice, corn, coos and cotton that were sometimes grown outside their huts. The Fula were regarded as the best farmers of millet and maize in The Gambia. To ensure fertility they tethered the cattle in the area they wanted to fertilise for over five or more nights before moving on. This manuring of the land took place especially before and during the rainy season. Salt mixed with certain leaves was usually administered to the cattle by the whole village. This ensured a healthy herd of cattle. Each morning the cattle were taken to the swamp for feeding and watering. The chief cattle owners in The Gambia were the Fula Firdu and Fula Kantora. Fula farmers also alternated certain types of coos. The harvested cotton was prepared into yarn by women for weaving Fula cloth. Farms passed from the male head to his successor.

Fig 7 - A Fula Woman.

46

Females and infants had no right to land. When land was hired the owners of the land had to tell what crops should be grown. Some women farmed swamp rice in the name of the family. There were professional hunters in every village. The Fula who stayed near the seas, swamps or rivers engaged in fishing.

With time some Fula settled in towns and cities and came to be considered townsmen. They became traders bartering or exchanging goods for local currencies.

FUTA TORO: AN EARLY FULA STATE

The first Fula state was Futa Toro, although this was not the original name of the state. It was called Tekrur and had developed into an empire under the ancestors of the Tukulor. Tekrur was ruled by the Ja-Ogo dynasty, said to be an Arab-Berber line of kings which had organised and ruled the people living in the kingdom for about 300 years. They were later conquered by a Mandinka dynasty known as the Manna (Manneh). It is believed that one of the princes of the Manna dynasty and ruler of the Tekrur Empire, War Jabi or Jabbi, was the first West African to be converted to Islam, and many of his subjects followed his example.

Tekrur grew rich, because its inhabitants took part in the trans-Saharan trade. This helped the state to develop into an empire located on both sides of the River Senegal. Between the eleventh and twelfth centuries, frequent revolts from its vassal states and dynastic struggles led the neighbouring empire of ancient Ghana to annex Tekrur. When the Almoravids attacked Ghana in 1076, Tekrur helped the invaders because they shared the same religion, Islam. With the fall of the Ghana Empire, the ruler realised his hopes of gaining the independence of Tekrur. But this freedom was short-lived because it became a vassal state, first of the ruler of Kaniaga, Sumanguru Konteh, in 1203 whose state in turn was brought under Sundiata Keita, ruler of the state of Kangaba, who defeated Sumanguru Conteh in the battle of Kirina in 1235. Sundiata Keita then laid the foundation of the ancient Empire of Mali and Tekrur remained a vassal state.

Around 1512, a Fula leader, Koli Tengella Bah, seized power from the reigning Manna dynasty and established the Denianke dynasty. He then changed the name Tekrur to Futa Toro with the first capital at Silla. The new ruler took the title *saltigi,* which means "Leader of the way". After the death of Koli Tengella in 1586, he was succeeded by one of his sons. The state adopted the patrilineal system of inheritance through the descendants of Koli. As his descendants increased, more and more people had the right to the throne, and this probably brought about the rotation of kingship among eligible families. A Council of Kingmakers, whose powers increased as candidates competed for power, elected kings. The members of the council often elected weaker candidates so that they could maintain power in their own hands. Later Futa Toro was probably divided into two kingdoms, Futa and Toro. At the height of their power, the kingdoms stretched from Senegal to the base of the Jalonke Region in present-day Guinea. The kingdoms were divided into many provinces that were ruled by chiefs who were under the authority of the saltigi. During the era of the Denianke dynasty, the Fula were dominant. There were also minority groups of Tukulor, Serer, Wolof, Mandinka, and Moors.

END OF FULA RULE IN FUTA TORO

One of the neighbouring groups of people that interfered a great deal in the politics of Futa Toro was the Moors. By the end of the seventeenth century, the saltigi's army included a large number of Moorish marabouts. The marabouts from Mauritania invaded this kingdom in the 1670s and controlled it until they were removed from power a few years later. The presence of the Moors led to constant struggles among people who were in favour of their stay and those against it. One of the rulers, Soulay Njie, tried to improve the situation by allocating land to certain people for cultivation. He enriched himself from the land rents received from his subjects. Other kings got their revenues from raids conducted on certain villages and also from tributes. Thus, this did not improve the situation, and the Denianke kings spent a good part of their time fighting with rebels in the provinces and repelling attacks from outside.

By the end of the eighteenth century, anarchy had set in and it was on the pretext of solving the interference from the Moors and re-establishing order that a Tukulor called Sulayman Bal rallied his people and started the Islamic revolution that brought an end to the Denianke dynasty. The last member of this dynasty moved to a village on the north bank of the River Senegal to continue his struggle against the Torodbe, the new Tukulor rulers. He was never able to get back his throne despite the fact that he defeated his enemies three times. Unfortunately for his people, he was killed in 1776, during the fourth encounter with his rivals. The death of the last member of the Denianke dynasty opened the way for Tukulor rule and domination of Futa Toro. Nevertheless, some Fula chiefs retained power in some of the provinces and their descendants who were not Muslims were converted to Islam. Also some of these Fula formed part of the council that elected the ruler or the *alimamy* of Futa Toro. The name alimamy was the new title of the Tukulor rulers.

FULA MIGRATION TO THE REST OF THE SENEGAMBIA REGION

Unlike other ethnic groups, which tended to settle in an area over a long period of time, the Fula continued to migrate to other places. As herdsmen, they were always in search of good pasture for their herds. Nomadic Fula were also regarded as stateless people because they did not establish governments nor did they settle in any one particular place. The families of nomadic Fula usually consisted of the father, his wives, and his children, moving from place to place, in search of good grazing land. In some cases, Fula villages were found along side those of other ethnic groups such as the Mandinka or Serahule as was the case in the Upper River Division of The Gambia. It is because of these movements that the Fula have over nine dialects reflecting different patterns of migration and acculturation with other African peoples; thus providing the wide but slight cultural differences that are apparent among them.

As they migrated into various parts of the Senegambia Region, some eventually settled in towns though most of them continued to wander around uniting themselves in kindred and family. Known for their migrations, some of the Fula intermarried and intermingled with peoples among whom they settled thus forming such acculturated groups as Mandinkanised Fula. Thus they were sometimes influenced by the people among whom they settled. Nevertheless they maintained their language, culture and tradition.

However, there were also true Fula who did not marry outside their groups and have not been influence by their contact with other groups.

The Fula also lived in clans. Sometimes several families of the same clan grouped together to help support one another, though there was little concentration of power. A group could decide to break up if the herd or the family became too large. Sometimes Fula villages replaced Mandinka ones as they migrated. Some of these Fula villages were founded by individuals and were named after the founders or heads of families. Examples of these were Sare Samba Cisse, Sare Pate and Sare Demba in the Casamance and Sare Abdou, Sare Sofi and Sare Bojo in the MacCarthy Island Division (now Central River Division) in The Gambia. Sare means village. Family bonds and lineages were strong having common Fula surnames or family names such as Jallow, Barry, Sowe, Kah and Bah among the Fula of Futa Toro, Futa Bundu, Futa Jalon and in the various places where they settled. Family names of the Firdu Fula included Baldeh, Jawo and Mbalow.

In the Wolof, Serer, and Mandinka states, settled Fula groups eventually had recognised leaders or rulers who acted as the link between the landlord and the Fula population within the settlements. These leaders were known as farba (or ardo). They were responsible for the collection of taxes and for settling disputes. Mandinka kings raided these chiefs when they feared that they were becoming too powerful, or too rich. The Fula population usually supported their chiefs when their positions were threatened. Fula society was stratified with the slaves at the bottom of the social ladder. However, Fula slave owners usually adopted their slaves and gave them their family names and this applied to purchased slaves and prisoners of war. Slaves were bought especially to augment the labour force in the families.

While Futa Toro and Futa Bundu in Northern Senegal could be considered the ancestral homes of the Fula because of their numerical strength, they continued to migrate to other parts of the region, settling in states like Jolof, Kayor, Baol and beyond. The Fula also migrated from Futa Toro and Futa Bundu to The Gambia settling in the Upper River Division into such states as Wuli, Sandu, Niani, and Kantora. They trekked over a hundred miles of the riverbanks, crossing from east and west.

The Fula from Futa Jalon in Guinea Conakry and Macina located south and west of the Great Bend of the Niger River in what is today Mali also migrated to The Gambia. A sub-group of the Fula, the Laobe, migrated from Kaja in Senegal to The Gambia to do wood working and produced wooden bowls, mortars and pestles for which they were well known.

The spread of Islam through jihads also influenced the migration of the Fula into the Senegambia Region. The jihads of the imamate of Timbo in Futa Jalon under the Fula, Karomoko Alpha in 1727-8 and that of Sulayman Bal in Futa Toro in the 1760s and 1770s, for example, encouraged the spread of the Islamic religion among non-Muslims in the Senegambia Region. Thus, these Islamic Fula states were always able to use the claim of wanting to spread Islam among traditional worshippers to invade other states. The Fula from the states of Futa Toro, Futa Jalon, and Futa Bundu also made frequent raids deep into The Gambia and into the other neighbouring states on the pretext of either helping their oppressed brothers or spreading Islam. The Fula in Futa Toro, Futa Bundu and Futa Jalon had embraced Islam and were determined to spread the religion and convert people. As stated in Chapter One, the desire to convert the traditional worshippers to Islam, was the main reason for the invasion of Kansala, the capital of the Kaabu Empire in 1868 that resulted in its disintegration. Many of the vassal states revolted and secured their independence. It was the Fula from Futa Jalon led by the Alimamy, Alpha Umar of Timbo, who helped the Fula man, Molloh Egue (Egge) Baldeh also known as Alfa Molloh, of the Mandinka state of Firdu to revolt against his overlord, the Mansa. He built yet another Fula kingdom known as Fulladu which developed into an empire in the south of the Senegambia Region. Alfa Molloh led them and became the new ruler of Firdu. He embarked on wars of conquest. He incorporated some Mandinka states of the former Kaabu Empire such as Sankolla, Geba, Tumanna, Wuropana, Pate, Kamako, Yega and Pating and thereby laid the foundation of the Fulladu Empire. After his death his son Musa Molloh Baldeh, who had accompanied him during some of the wars, continued to conquer many more states. He settled the Fula as he conquered new territories. He finally built the Fulladu Empire, which encompassed areas in the Upper River Division of The Gambia as far as Kayai Island, parts of Casamance and the eastern part of the former Portuguese Guinea which is presently Guinea Bissau. He stayed on the French side of his empire in Hamdallai but moved out in 1903, with his entire population of more than three thousand inhabitants to Kesser Kunda in the MacCarthy Island Division (now Central River Division) of The Gambia. He wanted to evade French control. Many Fula were established in places like the former Mandinka states of Jimara, Wuropana (or Eropana) and Kantora. In some instances Fula villages and towns even replaced Mandinka villages.

Although Musa Molloh was a Muslim and many of his people were Muslims, some held on to the traditional religion. In 1876 he however allowed the Catholic missionaries into British Fulladu and they were able to convert a few Fula. However many more were converted in Basse thus accounting for the few Fula who accepted Christianity.

END OF FULA INDEPENDENCE

Like the other states in this part of Africa, the Fula of the Senegambia Region became subjected to the Europeans, who used force or treaties of friendship or commerce to dominate them. Thus, Fula states the of Senegambia Region and even the nomadic Fula eventually came under European rule by the end of the nineteenth and early twentieth centuries. The Europeans, namely the French, British and Portuguese, were determined to control the Fula and succeeded in doing so.

The French eventually ruled Futa Toro, the ancestral home of the Fula that had earlier lost her independence to the Tukulor. However many of the Fula remained in the state. Fula states outside the Senegambia Region lost their independence to the Europeans. The French conquered Futa Jalon in 1896. Macina was first incorporated into the Tukulor Empire when the jihadist Al hajj Umar Taal executed their ruler Ahmad in 1862. The French, however, captured Macina from Al hajj Umar's son and successor Ahmad in 1893 and brought the Fula under their rule. In Northern Nigeria, the Sokoto Caliphate or empire which was established by the Fulani jihadist, Uthman dan Fodio, from 1795 onwards was eventually destroyed by the British in 1903.

Thus, up to the eve of 1918, it was only the Fula of the Fulladu Empire under Musa Molloh in the Senegambia Region that had maintained their independence from Europeans. This entailed a lot of diplomacy, of playing one European against the other and of signing treaties of friendship and co-operation by Musa Molloh to save his empire. But Musa Molloh did not escape European domination of his empire. His forced migration in 1903 from Hamdallai, the French side of his empire to Kesser Kunda in the MacCarthy Island Division (Central River Division) in The Gambia did not save the Fula from European domination. The British who accused Musa Molloh of slave dealing and of retaining taxes meant for them, arrested and deported him to Sierra Leone in 1919. He was allowed to return to The Gambia in 1923 but his position as ruler of British Fulladu was handed over to his son Cherno Baldeh in 1924. The Fula were finally placed under European rule as the Empire of Fulladu was divided into French, British and Portuguese Fulladu.

Political instability and the need for good grazing land led to the migration of the Fula from the Futa Toro, as far back as the thirteenth century, into the upper parts of The Gambia, the Wolof and Serer states in the western part of Senegal, Futa Jalon and as far as Cameroon. The desire to spread Islam was also another factor that led Muslim Fula to migrate. Thus, by the beginning of the twentieth century the Fula had dispersed through the length and breadth of West Africa.

5

THE TUKULOR

The Tukulor form the majority among the inhabitants of the middle Senegal River, in the area commonly known as Futa Toro, which is also regarded as their homeland. The Tukulor are also found in fairly large numbers in Mali, Guinea, Ivory Coast, and Burkina Faso (formerly Upper Volta). Sometimes they are regarded as Islamised Fula, though some people claim that they are a completely different ethnic group.

ORIGIN AND MIGRATION

The exact origin of the Tukulor is unclear, but it is known that they have had very strong links and similar culture with the Fula, sharing the same history and geographical zone and, to some extent, language. There is also the claim that the Tukulor are the outcome of intermarriages between the other groups like the Wolof and Serer who lived in the Senegal Region. A French writer claimed that their neighbours from the states of Jolof and Walo called them *Tokolor* and *Tokoror* respectively. The French version became Toucouleur. Some people claim that the Tukulor are the Torodbe Fula. The Tukulor themselves believe that the Tekrur Empire was established by their ancestors and that War Jabi was the first African ruler south of the Sahara to accept Islam. He, in turn, converted many of his subjects. The Tukulor were the first large group of West Africans to accept Islam, and allied themselves with the Almoravids to fight the jihad against their overlords, the rulers of the ancient Empire of Ghana. However, Tekrur was a vassal of the king of Mali, and when it gained its independence; it was under a Fula man called Koli Tengella as explained in Chapter Two. The Denianke dynasty which he established was overthrown by

54

Sulayman Bal who, by 1776, laid the foundation of the theocratic state of Futa Toro. This meant that the state was ruled according to the laws of God or that the officials were divinely guided. The new ruler took the title Alimamy, which means a religious leader; but in Futa Toro and some Muslim African states, it was also the title for the political-religious leader. The Tukulor became the pioneers in the evangelisation of the Western Sudan. They, like the Fula, undertook migrations from their homeland, Futa Toro. Since they were not a nomadic people their migrations were inspired by their desire to spread Islam and to find better land on which to settle and cultivate their crops. They were mainly agriculturalists; and when near seas and rivers, they engaged in fishing.

The desire to spread Islam and convert people led to the migration of the Tukulor into such places as the rest of Senegal, especially among the Wolof and Serer states, The Gambia, Mali and other countries in West Africa. For example, many Tukulor took part in the jihads of Northern Nigeria, where the Fulani leader Uthman dan Fodio overthrew the Hausa rulers in about 1804. However, the best known Tukulor in the spread of Islam was Al-hajj Umar Taal, who eventually established the Tukulor Empire in Western Sudan as he tried to spread Islam through jihads or holy wars. He was responsible for a large exodus of Tukulor from Futa Toro towards the Bambara and Serahule states, where he fought most of his wars. Also, in the latter part of the nineteenth century, the Tukulor continued to migrate to such states as Sine, Saloum, and the northern parts of The Gambia. Maba Jakhou Bah's migration and the spread of Islam by wars led to the establishment of yet another Muslim Tukulor state in Baddibu in the northern part of The Gambia. Many Tukulor Islamic leaders such as Al-hajj Umar Taal, Maba Jakhou Bah, Amadou Bamba Mbacke and Al-hajj Malick Sey came from Tukulor families, some of which include the Khan, Bah, Taal, Sey and Dem. These Islamic scholars spread Islam through jihads or by peaceful persuasion. They established Islamic centres of learning that attracted Muslims from the Senegambia Region and beyond. Children commenced the study of Arabic at the early age of four or five because Islam played an important role in the lives of the Tukulor.

TUKULOR STATES

Sulayman Bal's jihad in Futa Toro placed the Tukulor in power. These Muslims, referred to as the Torodbe, formed the new aristocracy of Futa Toro. Sulayman Bal's main objective was to bind the Torodbe in unity, discipline, and fraternity. These became the binding forces among the Torodbe, who originally were invariably of humble origin and who, in addition, aimed at spreading Islam.

But the troubles of Futa Toro were not over with the establishment of Torodbe rule. The Moors constantly raided the inhabitants. The new religious class was faced with constant opposition from the remaining members and supporters of the last ruling dynasty who sought to re-establish order. They observed with contempt that it was enough for a slave to learn to read the Koran in order to become a Torodo. The Fula regarded the Torodbe as power-seekers of humble origin. The Torodbe on the other hand, condemned their enemies as being uncivilized and animist, for not all Fula embraced Islam.

Fig 8 - A Tukulor Woman.

The effective leader of the state was the marabout, Abdul Kader Kan (Abd al-Qadir), because Sulayman Bal continued his wars against the Moors and other opponents of the Torodbe. When he was killed in 1770, Abdul Kader continued the struggle against their enemies. He eventually defeated the last saltigi of the Denianke dynasty, Suley-Bubu, in 1776. He enforced Islam as the state religion, seizing the land of those who refused to cooperate and rewarding victorious chiefs and warriors who furthered the spread of Islam. In the ensuing years, the Torodbe aristocracy replaced the Denianke and, in fact, owned most of the land. Abdul Kader built many mosques and collected taxes in accordance with the laws of Islam.

After reorganising Futa Toro, Kader embarked on wars aimed at converting his neighbours. He successfully attacked the Wolof state of Walo. However, he was not so successful with the people of Kayor, as he was defeated and made a prisoner of the ruler of Kayor. He was later released and sent away with the memory of his humiliating capture.

Back at home in Futa Toro, he was soon faced with more opposition from people who believed that his laws were too strict. He was eventually murdered in 1804. He was the first and only head of the state of Futa Toro, because after his death, the members of the Council of Kingmakers had greater power concentrated in their hands. They elected and deposed rulers at will. It was for this reason that Futa Toro was described as being ruled by a "theocratic oligarchy, which exerted great influence". This meant that the administration of the state was in the hands of the few but powerful members of the council, who ruled by the laws of the religion, in this case, Islam. Rulers were deposed for very minor reasons, especially if they appeared to be powerful. Thus, the alimamys were rulers only in name and invariably remained in power for periods of only one month to two years. During the ninety-seven years of religious regime, as many as fifty-one rulers came to power. However, one alimamy ruled for eleven different periods, ranging from four to six months. This showed that he had some influence over the members of the council. This type of situation caused a lot of political instability, for the council and the alimamys were always wrestling for power. Another Tukulor state, Bundu, was founded as late as the seventeenth century by a Tukulor man called Malik Sey (Sy). He had actually led a large number of Fula and Tukulor from the east of Futa Toro to Bundu, an area which was originally only sparsely populated with Mandinka, Serahule and Fula immigrants. Bundu became a powerful Muslim state. The rulers of Bundu took the title alimamy. There were seven alimamys from the time of Malick Sey, to the last ruler. Abdul Kader, the ruler of Futa Toro had interfered in the politics of Bundu by assassinating the ruler and replacing him with his own brother. But Kader's brother ruled for a very short time until he was removed from power by the brother of the dead king. In fact, it was believed that this brother took an active part in the assassination of Kader in 1804. The whole population of Bundu eventually accepted Islam, and this brought them into closer link with Futa Toro and Futa Jalon, another Fula-Muslim state to the south of Bundu.

The rulers took an active part in trade, since they had the advantage of being close to Bambuk, the gold producing area. This position made Bundu powerful among her neighbours, because the wealth she earned from the trade enabled her to buy guns and ammunition. Politically, Bundu was more stable than her sister states, Futa Toro and Futa Jalon. However, this stable situation was disrupted with the coming of the French.

Fig 9 - A Tukulor Man

The French methods of taking over the political control of the two main Tukulor states were completely different. In Futa Toro, they took advantage of the political instability and started erecting forts in different villages by the mid-nineteenth century. Between 1861 and 1869, they signed treaties with the rulers, and this placed the state of Futa Toro under French protection. By 1891 they had taken over complete political control of the whole state. Abdul Bokar Khan (Kan), the Almamy of Futa Toro was subjugated and later ruled by the Tukulor. He was faced with growing opposition at home and externally as well. This was because he imposed strict Islamic laws in Futa Toro and tried to spread Islam to the rest of the Senegambia Region. He opposed the emigration policy of Al-hajj Umar which encouraged Muslims to move out of European controlled areas, especially Futa Toro. Nevertheless he sympathised with African leaders like Alburi Njie, ruler of the state of Jolof and Amadu, (son of Al-hajj Umar Taal) ruler of the Tukulor Empire in their struggle against French domination. For example he gave shelter to the former and was corresponding with the latter on the possibility of a coalition against the French. The French plotted with Abdul Bokar Khan's enemies and exiled him from Futa Toro. He was eventually assassinated in 1891. Thus, Futa Toro, like the rest of the Fula states and empires of West Africa, was also placed under French rule.

In Bundu, on the other hand, the French tried to maintain friendly ties with the rulers. This led to the education of one of the sons of the reigning monarch, who later succeeded his father. He was called Bakari Sardu. With his French education, he was careful to keep on the French side. He made sure not to openly support the rivals of the French. On his death in 1886, the French took an active part in the politics of the state. They even placed a candidate on the throne who they felt would respond to their wishes, but he was removed from power by one of their opponents, Momodou Lamin Drammeh. The French eventually defeated him in The Gambia after a bitter struggle. Following this, Bundu came under French rule. Thus like the other ethnic groups the Tukulor suffered the inevitable fate of coming under European rule.

6

THE SERAHULE

The Serahule (Serahuli or Sarahule) are sometimes referred to as Soninke. Today they can be found in the present states of Mali, Senegal, Mauritania, Burkina Faso (formerly Upper Volta), Ivory Coast, Guinea-Bissau, and The Gambia. This group forms one of the minor ethnic groups in many countries. Yet the group is believed to be one of the oldest in West Africa.

ORIGIN

Like some of the ethnic groups of the Western Sudan, there is much controversy about the origin of the Serahule. One popular claim is that they originally came from the ancient Empire of Songhai, and were followers of the Sunni royal family who were forced into exile by the usurper, Askia Mohammed, in 1493. In exile they took the name Soninke, meaning "followers of Sunni". If this is true, then we can conclude that the Soninke or Serahule are a comparatively more recent group than such others as the Wolof or the Mandinka.

But the most popular claim is that the Soninke were, in fact, the ancestors of the Serahule, who were the main inhabitants of ancient Ghana Empire. They later gained influence in Ouagadougou (Wagadugu), the Soninke name for ancient Ghana. It is certain that the Soninke ruled this empire from about 777 A.D. until 1076 when it was conquered by the Almoravids. The members of the ruling class were known as *wago* (or *wage)* which the name Ouagadougou was derived.

According to tradition, the ancestor of the Serahule was a man called Dinga. Serahule legend claims that one of his sons built the capital of the ancient Empire of Ghana called Kumbi Saleh. However, he was helped by a huge serpent, which promised rain to the people five times a year in return for a yearly sacrifice of a young virgin. The legend further states that it also rained gold, which the inhabitants collected. The serpent was eventually killed by a young man who wanted to save a particular virgin about to be sacrificed to it. As a punishment for this deed, Kumbi Saleh had no rain for seven years, and the serpent's head was buried in Bure, a state later known for its gold. Although this is only a legend, it seeks to explain two things - why Ghana was so rich in gold that Arab chroniclers wrote about it, and why it later became a barren and desolate place. In the first instance, gold was so much in abundance that Al-Fazari described ancient Ghana as "the land of gold". Another writer, in his eager description, exaggerated when he said that "gold grew in the ground like carrots and was plucked at sunset". In any case, it is known that the gold did not come from Ghana itself but from the goldmines of Bure and Bambuk. Ghana obtained immense quantities of gold because it controlled the trans-Saharan trade routes and was in a position to accumulate gold from taxes collected on the goods that were exchanged in trade. An additional factor was that Ghana had a great advantage over her neighbours, in that it had iron and was therefore able to manufacture weapons with which wars of conquests were carried out. Consequently, vassal states such as Tekrur, Kaniaga and Kangaba, all paid tribute to ancient Ghana.

Secondly, the legend seeks to explain Ghana's long periods of famine which was due to the desiccation of the desert. Lack of rain dried up wells and greatly affected agriculture. When the Almoravids attacked the empire, which suffered a series of attacks from its former vassals, the area was reduced to desert by the destructive nature of the battles. Kumbi Saleh, the capital, once a flourishing city, had only a few mud huts left years later.

SERAHULE STATES

The attack of the Almoravids on the ancient Ghana Empire resulted in the large dispersal of the Serahule into the rest of the Western Sudan. Some were escaping from the wars and others from possible enslavement. However, Ghana did not come to its final end in 1076, even though it was at its weakest stage. The empire gradually declined after the Almoravids' attack. The people of Ghana became the vassals of Sumanguru Konteh, ruler of Kaniaga. This state, however, was razed to the ground at the Battle of Kirini in 1235 during the attack of the Mandinka leader, Sundiata Keita. Even before the final fall, migrations continued. What was once a powerful empire became a victim of constant raids. People therefore moved away in search of safer environments, better farmland and well-watered regions far away from the widening desiccation. Finally, the trans-Saharan trade routes shifted as a result of the wars. The Serahule were the middlemen of this trade. They therefore moved to areas where they could take better advantage of the trade. As a result, a new trading centre called Walata was built.

Typical Serahule men were a class of merchants who scarcely ever remained in their own country, but left their wives and children at home and went in search of trading goods. Some of these men could be considered as nomadic since they moved from state to state or town to town trading various types of goods. Thus they bartered goods like gold, hides and beeswax for European goods like blue bafts, guns, beads and gunpowder. These were again exchanged for salt, slaves, locally woven cloth and leather with traders in Bundu, Senegal, The Gambia or wherever they could make profits and depending on the desire of the clients. From the sixteenth to the early nineteenth centuries, the French and the British in both Senegal and The Gambia especially sought for gold and slaves. The former was used to mint coins and the latter for the plantations in the New World. As trading invariably enhanced their wealth, Serahule merchants gained the reputation of being rich. Thus when a merchant returned home from his trading expedition, it was the custom for his neighbours and friends to assemble to congratulate him. He then displayed his wealth and generosity by making a few presents to his friends. But if he was unsuccessful, then everyone looked on him as a failure, who after a long journey brought back nothing but the hair on his head. On the whole their clients regarded them as being fair and just in their trading.

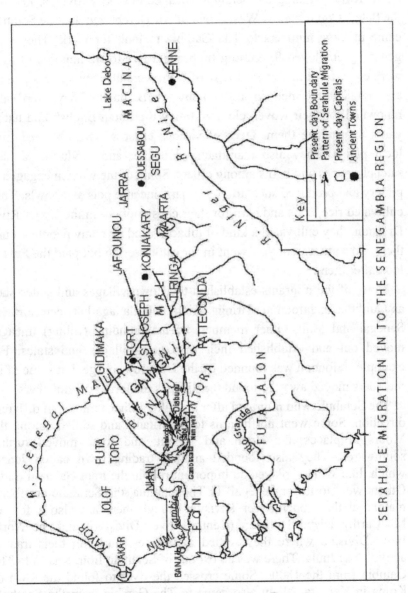

Map 7 - Some Serahule States and Migration Patterns

Apart from trading the Serahule engaged in other activities. In 1887, the Select Committee of West Coast of Africa reported that the Serahule came in large numbers to The Gambia to look for work. They were generally employed for cutting timber and five to six hundred of them were engaged in this work. Many of them were also engaged as pedlars and retail tradesmen in the colony of Bathurst. They were also renowned for their woven cloth and they used both English and native yarns to produce them. Dyes of various colours were obtained from local plants. They also manufactured leather and produced saddles, satchels, shoes and boots among others. Some of the women engaged in pottery and produced such articles as jars, incense pots and bowls. They cultivated rice, coos and corn for their consumption. In the Upper River Division, they cultivated a kind of tobacco used by many people around them. To some extent they went in for cattle rearing but paid the Fula to look after them.

Many of the migrants established their own villages and states such as Guidimaka, Jafounou, Tiringa, Kingi and Gajiaga between northern Senegal and Mali. Other members of the founding (ruling) lineages moved out and established their own new villages and states. For example, Jafounou was founded by the Dukuray lineage, but some of its members moved away to found the villages of Gori and Tambakara.

The Serahule who migrated after the fall of Ghana moved in different direction. Some went northwards to Mauritania and settled among the Moors in places like Hodh and Tagant; and some moved further southwards. They also founded another trading town called Jenne, which, like Walata, played an important role in the trans-Saharan trade. Others went to lower Senegal. In The Gambia, the Serahule are found mainly in the Upper River Division though there are also a few in MacCarthy Island Division (Central River Division) and the North Bank Division where they settled in villages, pursuing their trading activities as Juula. There was an exodus of Serahule from Kaarta to The Gambia from the 1800s. Some crossed the river to found the town of Koina in Kantora. Many also came to The Gambia from the Serahule states of Gajiaga, Guidimaka and Jafounou. Yet others came to The

Gambia during the religious wars of Momodou Lamin Drammeh against Bundu and the French. After his death, the Serahule who accompanied him settled in the Upper River Division in The Gambia. As the various groups of Serahule converged in the Central and Upper River Divisions, villages and towns such as Gambissara, Numuyel, Garawol and Alohungari were established.

As the Serahule settled among different peoples, they adopted the cultures and traditions of their hosts. They quickly adjusted to their new environment. In southern Mauritania, they soon became sedentary farmers, although they were always victims of constant Moorish raids. On the other hand, they sometimes influenced their hosts, an example being the name given to the major city in the Mossi area, Ouagadougou, which recalls the greatness of the first Serahule state.

Fig 10 A Serahule Woman

The Serahule never built another empire after Ghana. Apart from kings who succeeded to a limited extent in gaining control over a wide area, the rest of the Serahule states retained their independence. One particular factor prohibiting any expansion was the constant quarrels among the nobles, which led to civil wars. Weakened by these conflicts,

Kingi and the rest of the Serahule states were easy prey to other rising powers in the same region.

Around the 1880s, a Serahule marabout called Momodou Lamin Drammeh waged a jihad against unbelievers. His wars resulted in the building of an empire which incorporated many Serahule and Tukulor states. This empire extended as far as The Gambia with settlements founded there and in other parts of the empire too. The wars he embarked on led to the further spread of the Serahule in the Senegambia Region. Having had a near fatal contact with the French, he found his way to The Gambia with many of his Serahule followers. He was eventually killed there and these Serahule followers established their permanent homes in The Gambia.

END OF SERAHULE INDEPENDENCE

During the eighteenth century, the Bambara embarked on expansion and state building, and by the end of that century, they had conquered almost all the Serahule kingdoms and the surrounding states. The Serahule paid tribute to the Bambara rulers until 1854, when Al-haji Umar Taal waged a jihad not only against the Bambara states of Kaarta and Segu but also all states under Bambara rule. Thus, the jihadists did not engage the Serahule in direct confrontation although many of them had become laxed in their religious practices and could not escape the wars of Al-hajj Umar. He then placed his sons as governors of the various Serahule states even though the Serahule resented their new conquerors as much as they hated the Bambara rulers. There were as many revolts during the time of Al-hajj Umar as there were at the time of his son and successor Amadu. A more serious quarrel occurred between the Serahule marabout leader, Momodou Lamin Drammeh, and Ahmadu, the ruler of the Tukulor Empire. During this time many Serahule joined Lamin, though his attempt at fighting was foiled by the French.

Momodou Lamin was not the only one who fought the French. Ahmadu was also harassed by the French who were determined to capture his empire. Some Serahule kingdoms sided with the French since they were both fighting a common enemy, the Tukulor. At this point they regarded the French as their saviours, while the French regarded themselves as conquerors. A bitter struggle began between these two groups. Treaties were signed with the chiefs, forcing them to reduce the taxation of the traders and to abolish slavery. The French also wanted to build military posts, telegraph lines, railway lines, and roads across the states. When they tried to recruit labour for their various projects, the Serahule refused to cooperate with them and, as the struggle continued, hatred developed on both sides. In a particular dispute, a whole village was destroyed by the French, resulting in the death and wounding of countless villagers. The Serahule resented having their ancestral lands occupied by aliens. Moreover, they had a total dislike for non-Muslims, especially christianised ones like the French.

In the end, the French won. The chiefs were divested of all their powers and became middlemen between the French and the rest of their colonial subjects. Those Serahule who migrated to the Senegambia Region came under the jurisdiction of either the French or English at the time of the European partition of Africa.

7

THE JOLA

The Jola can be found in great numbers on the Atlantic coast between the southern banks of The Gambia, the Casamance Region of Senegal, and the northern part of Guinea-Bissau.

ORIGIN AND MIGRATION

Unlike the other ethnic groups of the Senegambia Region, there is very little known about the early history of the Jola. This is because they did not have griots in their traditions handing down the history of their ancestors from one generation to the next as with other ethnic groups. But it must not be concluded that the Jola did not have musicians and entertainers who delved into their past. The main difference was that among the Jola these talents were not bequeathed to succeeding generations, as was the case with other groups. For this reason, the oral histories of the Jola go back only two or three generations, in order to reconstruct the origin of a village or lineage of a family. Even where there is a history of a Jola group, it proves to be fragmentary. Another reason is that Europeans - traders, explorers, administrators and missionaries - provided scanty information about the Jola. It should be remembered that many of these Europeans remained mainly in the coastal areas. They rarely ventured into the areas inhabited by the Jola, mainly because numerous creeks, lagoons and swamps usually surrounded these places. As the Jola were often completely isolated from other ethnic groups, this made trade difficult and unprofitable.

Though the origins of the Jola are unknown, it is believed that they and other ethnic groups like the Bainounka, Balanta, Bassari and Pepel were already in the lower region of Casamance (and some parts of Guinea-Bissau) before the massive Mandinka migration of the thirteenth century. Some Jola, like other ethnic groups, became either assimilated in these areas or moved on to other places. Those who decided to migrate went northwards and westwards towards the Atlantic Coast, on the southern banks of the River Gambia. Some made Foni and Kombo their homes. The Jola of Foni called themselves Ajamat, a name believed to be applicable to all Jola people. The early European explorers who came to the coastal areas referred to them as the Feloops, Feloupes, Flouops, or Flups.

However, there is the possibility that some Jola and Serer migrated together from Kaabu situated in the Casamance region. It is not known where these people came from prior to their move from Kaabu. There is a tradition among both the Jola and Serer that their ancestors were travelling down the River Gambia in a canoe which split in two when they got to the area near Bathurst. The ancestors of the Jola hung on to the fore piece of the canoe and landed in the Kombo-Foni area while those of the Serer held tight to the other piece and were carried on to Barra, from where they moved and settled in the Sine and Saloum areas. Moreover those who remained in the Casamance Region also became known as the Jola, thus the joking relationship between these people.

The Jola are divided into many major groups, which are subdivided into smaller ones of which the family is the smallest unit. It is for this reason that the Jola have been regarded as having segmented groups and lineages. The various Jola lineages were located in different regions, villages, and settlements. This large dispersal of the Jola was due to both voluntary and forced migrations. A group of people within a larger group might decide to migrate because of overpopulation or because of the scarcity of land, and look for new areas to settle and to cultivate their rice or other produce. On the other hand, bloody conflicts took place over such issues as control of rice fields, and the defeated group moved away in search of areas for cultivation.

In Casamance in Southern Senegal and in parts of Guinea-Bissau, the major Jola groups or clans are Bliss, Karong, M'lomp, Elinkin, Cadjinol (the Jola of the Point Saint George area), Floup, Jamant, Djougout, Bayot, Brin, Seleky, Kabrouse, Jiwat and Fogny. However, in The Gambia Foni located on the southern bank of the river was occupied by a major group that came to be known as Jola Foni. Some also settled in

Kombo. These groups or clans were further subdivided into groups occupying certain zones and villages.

Groups of Jola resided in the area that stretched as far as Eassaont Jaken, Bou Kitingo, Emay, Nyanbalang, and Ayoun. Other Jola occupied areas in Guinea-Bissau with villages at Arame, Kerouhey, Suzanah and Kassalol as the main areas of settlement.

The Floup occupied several zones. They. were further divided into two large groups or clans known as Oussouye, which further broke into smaller villages. A second Floup group also founded several villages such as Arame, Suzanah, and Kassalol.

Another example of segments was the Jola Seleky who migrated from their original home, Nyassia, which they had shared with the Brin and Bayot Jola, to establish new villages in the mangrove swamps. There were further movements from various other groups that led to the establishment of more Jola lineages or villages. The Jola Kassa, Jembereng and Hitu had numerous large and small towns, villages and even families that settled independently.

This type of fission (breaking up) was a common happening among the Jola. The result was the creation of hundreds of large and small villages, each independent of the other with different dialects, depending on their environments and the people with whom they came in contact. The dialects of their language were invariably very different and although some claim similarities, sometimes one Jola group failed to understand the dialect of the other and one Jola culture and traditions were different from the others. In the area of religion, each group, lineage and family had its own god. Again this was due to the segmented nature of the Jola society.

Migrations were not well organised, nor did they involve large sections of the population as happened among the Mandinka, for example. Migrations involving larger numbers of people, towns, villages or families, for example, were often dictated by special happenings: When the head of the family or group died; when the land was believed to be cursed by diseases and frequent deaths; when there was believed to be cursed by diseases and frequent deaths; when there were three or four years of poor harvests, the stockades were destroyed and the people dispersed.

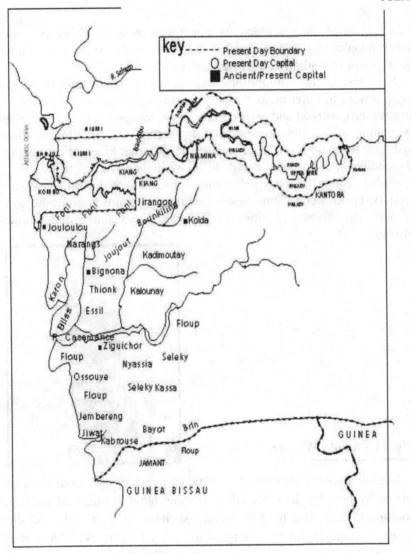

Map 8 - Some Major & Minor Jo Groups, Settlements & Towns

Some founded other settlements sometimes on vacant land or among other peoples, the Mandinka, for example, while others joined other Jola groups that admitted them as settlers.

But most of these migrations were seasonal. This meant that some people went to other areas for only a short while (normally during the dry season), worked and earned money, and returned in time to meet the beginning of the rainy season for the planting of rice. While on these seasonal migrations, the Jola engaged in different kinds of occupation, depending on what they could do or what they wanted to do. These included fishing, tapping palm wine, processing palm oil, harvesting oysters, cockles and clams, and sometimes engaging in domestic work in villages, towns and cities in Senegal, The Gambia and Guinea-Bissau.

Fig. 11 - A Jola Woman

Migrations were sometimes undertaken by groups of about the same age or by families. In some villages, some families migrated with few cooking utensils and built temporary shelters for their stay, and then returned home at the beginning of the rainy season. With time some Jola migrated permanently and eventually formed little colonies providing shelters and temporary help for new migrants from their original areas of residence, towns and villages. Others migrated to Niumi and Baddibu during the Soninke-Marabout wars when Foday Kabba Dumbuya, Foday Kombo Sillah and Ebrima Njie waged a series of wars against them in Foni, Kombo and northern Casamance. Others went to French Foni or other areas of The Gambia and Upper Senegal in search of better income and a better life. The British freed the Jola who were captured and enslaved either by the jihadists or traders and many settled in Bathurst and the Kombo. Others settled in Balangar and other Wolof villages and districts and adopted their culture and tradition. However by 1926 many Jola who had escaped to French Foni returned to British Foni after the jihadists were defeated by the Europeans.

Despite this breaking up of groups, clans and family, fusion (merging of units, groups and clans) also occurred among the Jola. Some of these groups or clans were broken into many large families which as a rule lived together thus when registering a group of stockades, the same names were found throughout. Such Jola families are the Kolley, Badji, Jarju, Sambou and Manga to name a few. There were also the Bojang, Camara, Sonko and Jammeh, which were probably from the Mandinka and showing close relationship with them. People of the same groups or clans say 'they are all of one breast', thus descendants of the same ancestors and are members of one family.

Sometimes a group of immigrants of another lineage may increase at the expense of the founding kinship group, which might supplant it as the dominant group. Clans, groups or families with ties of common descent linked segments of lineages scattered among a number of local communities. Sometimes they actually came together to strengthen a common position. A group of Jola of the same lineage and other Jola living nearby would unite and assist to drive an invader. Formerly, heads of scattered segments of lineages were summoned by the head of their senior branches for both ceremonial and practical affairs. Each lineage had a centre from which it originated and it had a grove of sacred trees said to be of ritual importance to all the members of the group. Later administrative force (for example the division of Jola land in French, British and Portuguese rule) and economic force and migrations appeared to have weakened the links of the Gambian Jola with their kinsmen as happened in other places throughout Jola country.

The towns were small and consisted of groups of compounds scattered some fifty to a hundred yards apart, surrounded by stockades.

Indeed, each town, village and sometimes family was fortified by stockades about eight to ten feet high, which were built with tree trunks and branches driven into the ground and sometimes filled with clay. These stockades were built to protect them from other Jola groups and clans and from outsiders. The Jola were invariably protected by forests and swamps and thus survived successive waves of intrusion in many areas, except on the banks of the River Gambia and along the Allahin (Hallahein) River at Kartong through which invaders reached the coast of Gunjur.

Sometimes small Jola settlements developed into villages and towns due to trade and/or migrations. In Foni, in The Gambia, some well-known towns were Kansala, Jarrol, Bondali, Kussamai and Karrenai. The Bainounka also occupied Jarrol, Kamessan, Kamandu and Kampasa. Bintang or Vintang, Brefet, Sibanor, Karrenai, Bondali and Bruman were among many other wharf towns and also important trading posts. Here the Portuguese, British and French traded with the Jola. Trade was also carried out around the streams of The Gambia and the sea on the Franco-British boundary between the Portuguese Creole of Ziguinchor and the Jola of Kombo whose principal villages were Kartong and Kalongo. The Mandinka were sometimes the middlemen of the trade. Sometimes the companies had factories with agents buying ivory, beeswax and slaves, some of which came from other parts of southern Gambia, Casamance and Guinea-Bissau. In Bintang they sold a good quantity of beeswax to the Europeans. The wax was collected from the woods. They also exchanged Manchester cotton for rubber.

By the 1880s, some Jola from Foni and parts of Kombo who were engaged in palm wine tapping migrated to St. Mary's Island, which was also Bathurst, the administrative capital. By the mid-nineteenth century more Jola migrated into other parts of the Senegambia Region and Guinea-Bissau. For example, thousands of Jola of southern Senegal which included the Kassa, Floup, Kabrouse and Jembereng migrated to The Gambia and settled in Kombo in Ebo Town, Jeswang and later the administrative capital Bathurst.

74

The Jola had no single king, paramount chief or overlord ruling all of them. Not even the towns had single headmen. Instead the owner or 'big man' of each stockade was his own king and recognised no one as being over him or having authority over him. The people living in his stockade obeyed him only as their superior. In Foni, the Jola had as many as seven hundred stockades and so-called headmen of groups of stockades were found but they had absolutely no power. Although now and again one came across a man to whose authority the people would submit, these were very few and far between. This demonstrated their love for independence. Some units obeyed only the head of the family who was the eldest male who was sometimes of the founding lineage. In Foni the Jola practised the patrilineal system of inheritance though other groups like the Kabrouse sometimes had female rulers and followed the matrilineal system.

The palm tree was important to the Jola. From this tree they tapped palm juice, which became palm wine or *bounouk* when left to ferment. Tapping was done from October to June, which is during the dry season, by adult males or youths twelve years and above. Palm wine was used for many activities such as marriages and funerals. People who were guilty of certain crimes were asked to pay certain quantities of palm wine. It became an important item of trade and was sold in many communities and in Bathurst (now Banjul). The palm oil used for cooking was produced from the fruit of the palm tree. The Jola, like the Wolof, used the palm oil for medicinal purposes. The Jola also collected kernel nuts that were sold to the Europeans. Since they used honey to make their own local liquor, they did not buy that brought in by the Europeans. Land was generally owned communally. A man in the village went into an area, cleared the land for himself and sought no permission from anyone to engage in farming. Women held no land but worked on the rice fields. Land in most areas where the Jola settled was fertile. They were and are still well known for their rice cultivation. The wealth of a typical Jola was measured by the quantity of rice he or she owned.

The Jola supplied rice to traders and exchanged it for cattle. They also produced large quantities of millet or coos and corn. When under European rule, they originally paid their taxes with a bundle of corn that was equivalent to three pence. Cotton and a small quantity of groundnuts were also grown.

From 1896 to 1902 the Travelling Commissioner reported that the Jola were gradually paying more attention to the production of the cash crop, groundnuts and by 1914-16 groundnut farms had extended extensively. Furthermore they grew watermelon, pumpkins, corn, sweet potatoes and yam. Other properties of the Jola included pigs, sheep, goats and cattle. These domestic animals were sometimes used for sacrifice. Cattle were so important to the Jola that they exchanged them for rice. Thus they usually had large numbers of cows though they were often reduced in number because of raiding from their neighbours. Cattle were important to the average Jola as they were slaughtered during initiation and funerals and used for the payment of fines. They had the custom of fattening animals for the above named events. They kept cap guns to ward off wild animals like lions and leopards that were common in the forest and for their funerals.

The products, such as the fish, palm wine, palm oil, rice, corn, oysters, cockles and clams were exchanged for other commodities of the local inhabitants and the rest used for consumption. Later when European currencies were introduced, the money derived from these occupations was used for buying clothes and other European goods and for the payment of taxes. In this way, the Jola met their other needs without selling all their rice.

The Jola did not have specific groups or families engaged in local industries like cloth weaving, leather work and gold and silver smith work as was evident among the Mandinka and Wolof for example. They invariably depended on these people or on Europeans for these products.

END OF JOLA INDEPENDENCE

The Jola were (and still are) proud of their independence and jealously guarded it against intruders. For this reason, they have been described as rebellious people who retained their independence at any cost. Their need for protection against any outside political control was determined by the nature of their society which had a segmented structure in all spheres of life.

During the period of the Soninke-Marabout wars in The Gambia between 1850 and 1890, marabout leaders like Foday Kabba Dumbuya, Foday Sillah, and Ebrima Njie carried out incessant raids on the Jola in their determination to convert them to Islam. Foday Kabba Dumbuya invaded Foni Jarrol and Bondali from which he collected tributes through agents installed in various centres. Foday Kombo Sillah captured such Jola villages as Abehney, Kujubeh, Jakalulu and those of the Bliss and Karong. Ebrima Njie was a Wolof jihadist whose headquarters was in Kombo. He also invaded western Foni, Bulufu and Bainounka countries in southern Casamance. Thus the independence of the Jola, especially those of Kombo and Foni in The Gambia and of northern Casamance, was put to an end. As a result of these wars, the Jola Foni (which was subdivided into about nine villages or settlements), the Jola Karong, and the Jola of Kombo all acknowledged the marabout leaders. The neighbours of the Jola to the east and west of Pakau and Yacine were the Mandinka from whom they experienced violent wars. But some of the Jola of these areas still held on to their traditional beliefs. Other Jola like those from the Kassa, Kabrouse, Her and Jembereng accepted Catholicism when missionaries followed traders into Casamance in the 1850s. Thus the work of the jihadists was incomplete.

The control of the marabouts was short-lived for they were defeated by the British and the French who wanted to put an end to these wars to help promote trade and gain political control of the region. The destruction of Foday Kabba Dumbuya by the French in 1894, for example, put an end to the hostilities without the submission of the Jola. In the end, the British took control of Foni and Kombo, and the French dominated the rest of the Casamance region. Although the Jola strongly resisted the French in some areas, French penetration at the beginning of the twentieth century was very slow and did not affect the lives of the people, especially those inhabiting the swamp and forest region. Some groups were aware of foreign control only when they were asked to pay taxes. Many Jola groups did not give up their independence to the foreign authorities. As late as 1942 the Floup revolted against the French, and this encouraged the Jola Kabrouse (Her) to follow suit the following year. This group of people who resisted the French was led by a priestess called Alinsitoe Jatta, who was later deported to

Timbuktu. For many years, the Jola Kabrouse harboured the belief that she would return and lead them again. Resistance to French occupation continued under various queens and kings for a period of time. Foni was made a British protectorate in early 1887 when Foday Kabba Dumbuya was raiding the people. In 1891 a commissioner appointed to delimit the Anglo-French boundary experienced many problems. Sitwell was appointed commissioner in 1893 and from thence administered Foni under the Protectorate System, first under Ordinance Number 11 of 1894 and later under Number 7 of 1902. This meant that Foni was forced to accept a commissioner and native tribunal. Serious cases such as murder, arson and manslaughter were to be dealt with by the Supreme Court of the colony. During colonial days Foni was divided into Foni East and Foni West districts. These were further divided into sub-districts. Foni East consisted of Bondali District with an identified chief with a native tribunal, and Kansala District which initially did not have a chief. The Travelling Commissioner sat as people did not trust their own headmen or newly imposed chiefs. Foni West consisted of Brefet District, Bintang District and Karrenai District

For some time the European powers were puzzled about ruling these people whom they regarded as aggressive and who were mostly without any recognized leaders. During Foday Kabba's rule, a number of Jola were incorporated as his trusted followers into the tribute levying systems of the areas that he conquered. The then seyfo (or chief) of Foni Kansala, for example, was brought up in Foday Kabba's household. Thus it seemed likely that the notion of territorial control and benefits in wealth and prestige derived from the position were effectively implanted among a few Jola during this period. The majority of the hitherto autonomous lineages and local communities equally resented this system of obeying a chief. This with the sentiments of traditional rights of various lineages to certain tract of the country led to considerable difficulty in establishing administrative districts of suitable size which would co-operate and respond to a single seyfo. Up to 1899 the Travelling Commissioner complained about the difficulty of getting to the stockades as Foni was different from other parts of the country. There were no large towns, no headmen and each family had its stockade and farm. Many would not even take a message to another stockade owner and the majority feared to give one. The crime rate was high. The commissioners were unable to make arrests because no Jola would arrest another and the Mandinka were afraid to do so. Some committed crimes in British Foni and fled to the French side and returned after the situation had calmed down. They did the same on the French side.

The proposed solution was the establishment of councils comprising the heads or other representatives of lineages traditionally associated with a number of areas from which the sefyo was selected by the European official. The British for example would be the first among equals. This, however, depended on the full investigation of the lineage organisation of the Jola and whether there were means of associating them together in a wider organisation. The British did not conquer the western end of Foni nearer Bathurst and they therefore refused to pay taxes for several years and sometimes even insulted the commissioner.

Thus at the beginning of their administration, both the French and the British used the Mandinka to provide a link between them and the rest of the Jola population. The newly installed Mandinka chiefs also collected taxes and assisted in the administration of the various regions.

For some time the Jola, especially the heads of the traditional religions, tried to resist the Europeans; but like many other ethnic groups in West Africa, they came to realise that it was useless to fight the foreigners who had superior weapons. Nevertheless, they resented European rule as they did that of the Mandinka rulers. After 1900 the commissioner reported of the gradual acceptance of their presence. For example the people on the east end of Foni paid two shillings a stockade, some having about fifteen houses. By 1903-4 the Jola had become friendlier and even went to the commissioner with problems. After this period, the Casamance region was divided into districts. Mandinka chiefs were gradually replaced by Jola who had received French education and could therefore speak the language.of the colonialists In the end, the Jola gradually became more amenable to foreign rule. Thus, like other ethnic groups of the Senegambia Region, the Jola lost their freedom to the European colonialists, which lasted until the modern states of Senegal and The Gambia obtained their independence from France and Britain in 1950 and 1965 respectively.

Bibligraphy

Abbreviations

ANS. Archives Nationales du Sénégal
BIFAN. Bulletin de l'Institut Fondamental de l'Afrique Noire
GNA. Gambia National Archives
IFAN. Institut Fondamental de l'Afrique Noire

Books

Ajayi, J. F. Ade & Crowder Michael, (eds). *History of West Africa vol 1* (Third edition) . Longmans Group Ltd London, 1992.

Ajayi, J. F. Ade &Cowder Micheal, (eds) *History of West Africa. vol 11* (Second edition). Longmans Group Ltd. London, 1987.

Archer, Francis Bisset. *The Gambia Colony and Protectorate. An official Handbook.* Frank Cass & Co.Ltd. 1967.

Ba, Oumar. *Les Peul du Djolof (Sénégal) au XIX Siècle.* IFAN. Dakar. 1970.

Baa, Tamsir. *Essai Sur le Rip Sénégal* BIFAN T XIX Sr. B No. 3-4. 1957.

Barry, Boubacar. *Le Royaume de Waalo: Le Sénégal Avant le Conquête.* François Maspero. Paris. 1972.

Bathily, Abdoulaye. *A Discussion of the Tradition of Wagadu with Some References to Ancient Ghana, Including a Review of the Oral Account, Arabic Sources and Archaeological Evidence.* BIFAN T 37 sr. B no 1-2. 1975.

Bathily, Ibrahima. *Notice Socio-historiques sur l'Ancient Royaume Soninke du Gadiaga.* BIFAN T XXXI S No I. 1960.

Becket, C et Martin, V. *La Kayor et Les Payes Voisins au Cour de la Seconde Moitié du XVIII Siècle.* Mémoire inédit du Doumet (1769). BIFAN T. XXXVI. ser. B. n° 1, 1974.

Charles, Eunice A. *The Jolof Kingdom 1800-1890.* Boston University Press. Boston 1977.

Cissoko, Sekene Mody. *La Royaute (Mansaya) Chez les Mandigues Occidentaux d'après leur Tradition Oral.* BIFAN XXXI NO. 2. 1968.

Cissoko, Sekene Mody. *Introduction a l'Histoire des Mandigues de l'Ouest: L'Empire de Kabou. (XVI-XIX SIECLE)* Conference on Manding Studies, School of Oriental & African Studies. University of London. London. 1972.

Cleary, Michael Fr. *Reaping a Rich Harvest.: A History of the Catholic Church in The Gambia.* New Type Press. Banjul. 1990.

Diallo, Thierno. *Le Gaabu et le Futa Jalon, Colloque International Sur Les Traditions Orales du Gabou.* Dakar. 1980.

Diop, Abdoulaye. *Enquête Sur la Migration Toucouleur à Dakar.* BIFAN T XXII Sr. B no 3-4. 1960.

Diop, Abdoulaye B. *Société Toucouleur et Migration*. BIFAN T XXII Sr. b.no 2-3. 1965.

Diop, Abdoulaye Sokhna. *L'Impact de la Civilisation Manding au Sénégal: La Génése de la Royaute Gueleware au Siin et au Saalum*. BIFAN T XX Sr, B no 3-4. 1978.

Diop, Abdoulaye-Bara. *La Faimille Rurale Wolof:Mode de Résidence et organisation Séocio-economique*. 1974.

Gailey, H. A. *History of The Gambia*. Routledge and Kegan Paul, London. 1964.

Galloway, Winifred. *A Listing of Kaabu & some States and Associated Areas: Signpost Towards State by States Research in Kaabu*. OHAD. Banjul. 1980.

Galloway, Winifred. *History of Wuli*. (Unpublished thesis) University of Illinois. 1978.

Galloway, Winifred. *The Oral Traditions of Kaabu: An Historical Essay on Some Problems Connected with their Findings, Collections, Evaluation and Use*. OHAD, Banjul. 1980.

Gamble, D.P. *The Wolof of Senegambia*. London. 1957.

Gray, J.M. *A History of The Gambia*. Frank Cass & co. Ltd. London. 1966.

Mane, Mamadou. *Contribution à l'Histoire du Kaabu, des Origines au XIX Siècle*. BIFAN T 40 Ser. B no 1. 1978.

Mark, Peter. *The Wild Bull and the Sacred Forest.: Form, Meaning, and Change in Senegambia Initiation Masks*. Cambridge University Press. Cambridge. 1992.

Martin et Becker, C. *Lieux de Culte et Emplacement Célébres dans les Pays Serer (Sénégal)* BIFAN 41 Ser B no 1. 1978.

Reeve, Henry F. The Gambia. London. 1912.

Robinson, David. *Abdul Bokar Kan. Chiefs and Clerics: Futa Toro 1853-1891*.Oxford University Press, Oxford. 1975.

Sidibe, B. K. *The Nyanchos of Kaabu*. OHAD. Banjul. 1980.

Sidibe, B K. *Migration and Settlement of Early Kaabu States*. OHAD. Banjul. 1980

Sonko-Godwin. Patience. *Leaders of the Senegambia Region: Reactions to European Infiltration. 19th –20th Century*. Sunrise Publishers. Banjul. 1995.

Sonko-Godwin Patience. *Social and Political Structures in the Pre-colonial Period*. Sunrise Publishers. Banjul. 2000

Thomas, L-V 1961. *La Frustration Chez les Diola (Enquête Préliminaire)*. BIFAN T XXIII no 3-4.

Thomas, L-V. 1960. *Esquisse sur les Movements de Populations et Contact Socio-Culturel en Pays Diola (Basse Casamance)* BIFAN XXII no 3-4.

Thomas, L-V. *Les "Rois" Diola Hier, Aujourd'hui et Demain*. BIFAN T XXII. No 1-2

Ukpabi. S. C. *The Gambia Expedition of 1901*. BIFAN T. XXXII Ser. B no 2.

Wane. Mamadou.1977. *Les Toucouleru de Fouto Tooro (Senegal)* BIFAN T XXXIII Ser. B. no 4.

Documents

1G 33 (1) *Migration Kaabuke Pays Serer*.
(2) *Extraite de la Notice sur les Sereres (1800-1871)* par Pinet Laparde. ANS
1G 33b (1) *Notices sur les Serer et le Diander*.

(2) *Note sur le Diander et les pays des Serers Nones (a la suite des expédition de 1861)* Par Pinet Laparde 1861. ANS.

1G 34. Exploration de la Haute Casamance et des Rivières. 1866. Voyage de M. Vallon. ANS.

1G 75. *La Siège de Kansala.* Extraite de Loitard.

Colonial Office. *Llewelyn's Report 1896-1998. Memorandum - Proceedings of Interview with Musa Molloh.* GNA.

NGR 1/15. *Jola Tribe.* GNA

NGR 1/16. *Serahule Tribe.* GNA.

NGR 1/24. *Wolof Files.* GNA

NGR 1/31. *Gambian Fula.* GNA

CSO 2/45. *Report of Travelling Commissioner, Upper River Division. To The Honourable Colonial Secretary. Borabo. 2nd July 1903.* By W.B. Stanley. GNA.

CSO 2/151. *Diary of the Commissioner North Bank Province for 1901.* GNA

CSO. 2/1064 . *History of Kantora.* GNA.

Glossary

Abbreviations of names of ethnic groups:
(M) - Mandinka, (W) -Wolof, (S) - Serer, (F) - Fula, (T) - Tukulor, (Ser) -Serahule
J- Jola.

Aku, descendant of Liberated Africans, many of whom came from other parts of West Africa.

Alimamy, title of the rulers of Futa Toro under Tukulor rule

Alkalo, (M) name of a Mandinka village chief.

Balafon, (M) Xylophone.

Badola, (W) peasants.

Bolombato, (M) a gourd harp.

Bounouk (J) name for palm wine.

Bur, (W, S) Title of the kings of the Serer States of Sine and Saloum.

Bur Jullit (W) Name given to Muslim rulers in the Wolof states

Cherreh, (Ser) cereal made from millet or coos flour.

Coos. Millet.

dalii, (M) prediction made by the Emperors of the Kaabu Empire before the commencement of their rule.

dankuto, (M) – Joking relationship between two lineages or groups of people. They swore to go to each other's assistance in times of trouble, mediate on behalf of each other without causing offences, and intermarry.

dyula (M) trader (French spelling)

Gelwar, (M) Name of Mandinka rulers who settled in Sine and Saloum.

griots, Name used by Europeans to refer to traditional historians, genealogists and praise singers.

Guelewar. (M) See Gelwar.

jalang, (M) The traditional ancestral religion and places of worship.

juula, (M) Trader (English spelling)

kabilo, (M) A lineage.

kankurang ,(M) Masquerades used by the peoples of the Senegambia Region especially the Mandinka, for example the *fara kankurang* (for initiation) and the *jamba kankurang* (for festivals, marriages and aming ceremonies).

kontingo (M) A musical instrument of the ancient Kaabu Empire.

kora, (M) a twenty-one-string musical instrument used by the Mandinka griots.

Korings, (M) Nobilities of the ancient Kaabu Empire

Lamans, (W) Village chiefs

Linger, (W) Queen/noble women

Mamoo, (M) A masquerade that came out during female initiation.

Nyanchos, (M) Nobilities of the ancient Kaabu Empire

Saltigi, (F) Title of the ruler of Futa Toro

Seefoo/seyfo (M) Head chief

tata/tato (M) Fortress

tinirinya (M) Masquerade of the ancient Kaabu Empire.

Torodbe, (T) (Torodo Singular) Tukulor scholars engaged in the study of the Koran.

Toubanan, (W) From the Wolof word toub meaning convert, this was the nickname given to Muslim invaders of the Wolof States

Wage/Wago, (Ser) Ruling class among the Soninke, the ancestors of the Serahuli.

Index

A

Ajamat, 69
Al-Fazari, 61
Al-kanemi, 16
Almany, 49, 51, 55, 57 - 59
Almoravids, 3, 23, 47, 54, 60
Atlantic trade, 25, 27
Arab chroniclers, 61, 62
Ardo 50
Awdagost, 23

C

cash crop, 28, 36, 76
cattle breeding, 43
cattle herders, 42, 43
Ceesay, Biram, 16, 40, 76
cherreh, 34
Councilors of Kingmakers, 48, 57
cow dung, 43
crocodiles, 48, C
Customary taxes, 29, 30

D

dalii, 13
Dinga, 60
dankuto, 7
Drammeh, Momodou Lamin, 57, 65-67

dual kingship, 26
Dumbuya, Foday Kabba, 16,
   17, 72, 77, 78

E

European/s, 1, 11, 17-21, 25, 27-28, 30-31,
38,40, 44, 52-53, 59, 62, 67-69, 73-76, 78-79

B

badola, 27
Bah, Koli Tengella, 25, 48, 54
Bah, Maba, Jakhou, 16, 34, 37-40,
   55
Bal, Sulayman, 49, 1, 55-57
balaba
balafon 8
Baldeh, Alfa Molloh Egue 14,
   51, 52
Baldeh, Cherno 53,
Battle of Kansala ,13,
Battle of Kirina, 47, 52
Battle of Somb, 39
bolombato 8
Boure 32
Bubakar, Amadu 24
Bubu Suley 57
buur 33
Buur Jullit 26

F

Faal, Latir Sukaabe 26
Faal, Samba Laobe 37 - 39

Faatim-Penda, Birayma 34
Fak, Leeli Fuli 26
Faidherbe, Louis 30, 31, 37
farba 50
Fodio, Uthman Dan 16, 53, 55
forced labour, 18
Fula, Islamised 54
Fula, Mandinkanised 50

G

gelwar 33, 34
genii 24
God, 55
gold, 61
griots 11
gunpowder stores, 14

H
holy wars, 55
34, 72, 76

I

Islamic centres, 55
Islamic Laws, 59
Islamic revolution, 49
Islamic scholars 55

J

Jabi, War 47, 54
jalang 13
jali 11
Jatta, Alinsitoe 77
Jihadists, 66, 73, 77
Jihads, 15, 16, 23, 26, 37, 54, 56, 66
Jobe, Lat Jor 31
Jobe, Yerim Mbanyik Anta 25
Joof, Kodu 34, 38, 39
Jon, Mansa Wali 24, 33
juula 11, 65

K

kaabiiloo 11, 12
Kaabu-Futa Jalon War, 15
Kan, Abdul Kader 57, 59
Kangaba 3, 47, 61
Kani, Nderi 16
Kaniaga, 3, 47, 61, 62
Kankurang, 8
Kansala 5, 12, 14, 15, 51
Keita, Sundiata, 3, 4, 20, 47, 62
King of Pachana,
King of Saloum, 39, 40
King of Sine, 24, 39
Konteh, Sumanguru 3, 47, 62
Kontingo, 8
Kora, 8
Korings, 7, 8

L

lamans, 20, 23, 33
laws of Islam, 57
linger 30
lingua franca 19

M

Malek, Mbody 29
Mamoo, 8
Manding, 3
Maty, Sait 16, 40
Mbacke, Amadou Bamba, 55
Mboge, Guedel, 40
Mohammed, Askia, 60
Molloh, Musa, 53
Muhamed, Abu Bakr Ibn 23

N

Native tribunal, 18, 78
Ndari, Mamur, 16, 40
Ndaw-Njie, Birayamb Ma-Dyign
Ndure, Kumba Ndoffen, 38
Ndure, M'began 33
Njie, Alburi 31, 59
 26
Njie, Ebrima 72, 77
Njie, M'bake Deb 40
Njie, Njanjan 23, 24
Njie, Souley 48
Ngone, Ma Isa Bige 26
Njombot, Princess 29, 30
Nyanchos 7, 8, 32, 33
Nyancho Women, 14

O

Ozanne 17

P
palm wine, 28, 75, 76
partitioning of Africa, 17, 67
People, stateless 49

R

Relationship, joking 7, 12, 15, 69
River, Hallahein 74
Rule, Indirect 17, 31
rulership, dual 21

S

Sal, Fatimata 23
Salleh, Kumbi 61
Saltigi 48, 57
Sama, King of 12 - 14
Sanneh, Janke Wali 13, 14
Sanneh, Kelefa 12
Sardu, Bakari 59
Sey, Al-hajj Malick 55, 58
Sillah, Foday Kombo 16, 17, 72,
  77
Sitwell, 78
Sobel, Amari Ngone 26
Soninke-Marabout Wars, 15, 17,
Songhai, 60
stockades 70, 73 - 75, 78, 79
Sunni royal family, 60

T

Taal, Al-hajj Umar 16, 53, 55, 59, 66
Tarawally, Tiramang 4, 5, 7
tata, 13
tato, 13
Tekrur 47, 54, 61
territorial expansion, 30
theocratic oligarchy 57
tinirinya, 8
toubanan, 26
trade, trans-Saharan 4, 13, 47,
  61, 62, 64
Travelling Commissioners, , 17

U

Umar, Alpha 51

W

Wade, Barka Mbody 24
Wago, 60
West Indian Regiment, 16
Wolof, 19-28,31, 33-34, 37,42-43, 48,
   50, 53-55, 57, 60,73, 75-77
Wuropana, 5, 10, 17 52

Y
Yalla, Ndate 29, 30

Printed in the United States
by Baker & Taylor Publisher Services